SCIENCE
FUSION

fusion [FYOO • zhuhn] a combination of two or more things that releases energy

This **Interactive Student Edition** belongs to

_____

Teacher/Room

_____

HOLT McDOUGAL

 HOUGHTON MIFFLIN HARCOURT

Consulting Authors

Michael A. DiSpezio

Global Educator
North Falmouth, Massachusetts

Michael DiSpezio is a renaissance educator who moved from the research laboratory of a Nobel Prize winner to the K–12 science classroom. He has authored or co-authored numerous textbooks and written more than 25 trade books. For nearly a decade he worked with the JASON Project, under the auspices of the National Geographic Society, where he designed curriculum, wrote lessons, and hosted dozens of studio and location broadcasts. Over the past two decades, he has developed supplementary material for organizations and shows that include PBS *Scientific American Frontiers, Discover* magazine, and the Discovery Channel. He has extended his reach outside the United States and into topics of crucial importance today. To all his projects, he brings his extensive background in science and his expertise in classroom teaching at the elementary, middle, and high school levels.

Marjorie Frank

Science Writer and Content-Area Reading Specialist
Brooklyn, New York

An educator and linguist by training, a writer and poet by nature, Marjorie Frank has authored and designed a generation of instructional materials in all subject areas, including past HMH Science programs. Her other credits include authoring science issues of an award-winning children's magazine; writing game-based digital assessments in math, reading, and language arts; and serving as instructional designer and co-author of pioneering school-to-work software for Classroom Inc., a nonprofit organization dedicated to improving reading and math skills for middle and high school learners. She wrote lyrics and music for *SCIENCE SONGS,* which was an American Library Association nominee for notable recording. In addition, she has served on the adjunct faculty of Hunter, Manhattan, and Brooklyn Colleges, teaching courses in science methods, literacy, and writing.

Acknowledgments for Covers

Front cover: *Fiber-optic cable* (bg) ©Dennis O'Clair/Stone/Getty Images; *pacific wheel* (l) ©Geoffrey George/Getty Images; *snowboarder* (cl) ©Jonathan Nourok/Photographer's Choice/Getty Images; *water droplet* (cr) ©L. Clarke/Corbis; *molecular structure* (r) ©Stockbyte/Getty Images

ISBN 978-0-547-58943-5

17 18 19 20   0029   21 20 19 18

4500697186   DEFG

Michael R. Heithaus

*Director, School of Environment
and Society
Associate Professor, Department of
Biological Sciences*
Florida International University
North Miami, Florida

Mike Heithaus joined the Florida International University Biology Department in 2003. He has served as Director of the Marine Sciences Program and is now Director of the School of Environment and Society, which brings together the natural and social sciences and humanities to develop solutions to today's environmental challenges. While earning his doctorate, he began the research that grew into the Shark Bay Ecosystem Project in Western Australia, with which he still works. Back in the United States, he served as a Research Fellow with National Geographic, using remote imaging in his research and hosting a 13-part *Crittercam* television series on the National Geographic Channel. His current research centers on predator-prey interactions among vertebrates, such as tiger sharks, dolphins, dugongs, sea turtles, and cormorants.

Donna M. Ogle

Professor of Reading and Language
National-Louis University
Chicago, Illinois

Creator of the well-known KWL strategy, Donna Ogle has directed many staff development projects translating theory and research into school practice in middle and secondary schools throughout the United States. She is a past president of the International Reading Association and has served as a consultant on literacy projects worldwide. Her extensive international experience includes coordinating the Reading and Writing for Critical Thinking Project in Eastern Europe, developing an integrated curriculum for a USAID Afghan Education Project, and speaking and consulting on projects in several Latin American countries and in Asia. Her books include *Coming Together as Readers; Reading Comprehension: Strategies for Independent Learners; All Children Read;* and *Literacy for a Democratic Society.*

Program Reviewers

Content Reviewers

Paul D. Asimow, PhD
*Professor of Geology
and Geochemistry*
Division of Geological and
Planetary Sciences
California Institute of Technology
Pasadena, CA

Laura K. Baumgartner, PhD
Postdoctoral Researcher
Molecular, Cellular, and
Developmental Biology
University of Colorado
Boulder, CO

Eileen Cashman, PhD
Professor
Department of Environmental
Resources Engineering
Humboldt State University
Arcata, CA

Hilary Clement Olson, PhD
Research Scientist Associate V
Institute for Geophysics, Jackson
School of Geosciences
The University of Texas at Austin
Austin, TX

Joe W. Crim, PhD
Professor Emeritus
Department of Cellular Biology
The University of Georgia
Athens, GA

Elizabeth A. De Stasio, PhD
*Raymond H. Herzog Professor
of Science*
Professor of Biology
Department of Biology
Lawrence University
Appleton, WI

Dan Franck, PhD
Botany Education Consultant
Chatham, NY

Julia R. Greer, PhD
*Assistant Professor of Materials
Science and Mechanics*
Division of Engineering and
Applied Science
California Institute of Technology
Pasadena, CA

John E. Hoover, PhD
Professor
Department of Biology
Millersville University
Millersville, PA

William H. Ingham, PhD
Professor (Emeritus)
Department of Physics and
Astronomy
James Madison University
Harrisonburg, VA

Charles W. Johnson, PhD
*Chairman, Division of Natural
Sciences, Mathematics, and
Physical Education*
Associate Professor of Physics
South Georgia College
Douglas, GA

Program Reviewers *(continued)*

Tatiana A. Krivosheev, PhD
Associate Professor of Physics
Department of Natural Sciences
Clayton State University
Morrow, GA

Joseph A. McClure, PhD
Associate Professor Emeritus
Department of Physics
Georgetown University
Washington, DC

Mark Moldwin, PhD
Professor of Space Sciences
Atmospheric, Oceanic, and
Space Sciences
University of Michigan
Ann Arbor, MI

Russell Patrick, PhD
Professor of Physics
Department of Biology,
Chemistry, and Physics
Southern Polytechnic State
University
Marietta, GA

Patricia M. Pauley, PhD
Meteorologist, Data Assimilation Group
Naval Research Laboratory
Monterey, CA

Stephen F. Pavkovic, PhD
Professor Emeritus
Department of Chemistry
Loyola University of Chicago
Chicago, IL

L. Jeanne Perry, PhD
Director (Retired)
Protein Expression Technology
Center
Institute for Genomics and
Proteomics
University of California, Los
Angeles
Los Angeles, CA

Kenneth H. Rubin, PhD
Professor
Department of Geology and
Geophysics
University of Hawaii
Honolulu, HI

Brandon E. Schwab, PhD
Associate Professor
Department of Geology
Humboldt State University
Arcata, CA

Marllin L. Simon, Ph.D.
Associate Professor
Department of Physics
Auburn University
Auburn, AL

Larry Stookey, PE
Upper Iowa University
Wausau, WI

Kim Withers, PhD
Associate Research Scientist
Center for Coastal Studies
Texas A&M University-Corpus
Christi
Corpus Christi, TX

Matthew A. Wood, PhD
Professor
Department of Physics & Space
Sciences
Florida Institute of Technology
Melbourne, FL

Adam D. Woods, PhD
Associate Professor
Department of Geological
Sciences
California State University,
Fullerton
Fullerton, CA

Natalie Zayas, MS, EdD
Lecturer
Division of Science and
Environmental Policy
California State University,
Monterey Bay
Seaside, CA

Teacher Reviewers

Ann Barrette, MST
Whitman Middle School
Wauwatosa, WI

Barbara Brege
Crestwood Middle School
Kentwood, MI

Katherine Eaton Campbell, M Ed
Chicago Public Schools-Area 2
Office
Chicago, IL

Karen Cavalluzzi, M Ed, NBCT
Sunny Vale Middle School
Blue Springs, MO

Katie Demorest, MA Ed Tech
Marshall Middle School
Marshall, MI

Jennifer Eddy, M Ed
Lindale Middle School
Linthicum, MD

Tully Fenner
George Fox Middle School
Pasadena, MD

Dave Grabski, MS Ed
PJ Jacobs Junior High School
Stevens Point, WI

Amelia C. Holm, M Ed
McKinley Middle School
Kenosha, WI

Ben Hondorp
Creekside Middle School
Zeeland, MI

George E. Hunkele, M Ed
Harborside Middle School
Milford, CT

Jude Kesl
Science Teaching Specialist 6–8
Milwaukee Public Schools
Milwaukee, WI

Joe Kubasta, M Ed
Rockwood Valley Middle School
St. Louis, MO

Mary Larsen
Science Instructional Coach
Helena Public Schools
Helena, MT

Angie Larson
Bernard Campbell Middle School
Lee's Summit, MO

Christy Leier
Horizon Middle School
Moorhead, MN

Helen Mihm, NBCT
Crofton Middle School
Crofton, MD

Jeff Moravec, Sr., MS Ed
Teaching Specialist
Milwaukee Public Schools
Milwaukee, WI

Nancy Kawecki Nega, MST, NBCT, PAESMT
Churchville Middle School
Elmhurst, IL

Mark E. Poggensee, MS Ed
Elkhorn Middle School
Elkhorn, WI

Sherry Rich
Bernard Campbell Middle School
Lee's Summit, MO

Mike Szydlowski, M Ed
Science Coordinator
Columbia Public Schools
Columbia, MO

Nichole Trzasko, M Ed
Clarkston Junior High School
Clarkston, MI

Heather Wares, M Ed
Traverse City West Middle School
Traverse City, MI

Contents in Brief

What do water ripples and sound from a trumpet have in common? They are both waves that spread out from their sources.

Contents

Have you ever felt the vibrations when music is played loudly? Sound waves can make things, like this megaphone, vibrate.

Energy can travel through water as waves. The greater the amount of energy in a wave, the taller and more destructive the wave can be when it reaches shore.

Do you know a DJ? Disc jockeys, or DJs, rely on their knowledge of sound waves to "mix" music.

Assignments:

_____

_____

_____

_____

_____

_____

_____

Contents (continued)

This astronaut's helmet has a special gold coating. The coating allows the astronaut to see while protecting him or her from harmful sun rays.

© Houghton Mifflin Harcourt Publishing Company • Image Credits: ©NASA

Assignments:

_____
_____
_____
_____
_____
_____
_____
_____
_____
_____
_____
_____
_____
_____
_____
_____
_____
_____
_____
_____
_____
_____

Power up with Science Fusion!

Your program fuses. . .

e-Learning and Virtual Labs

Labs and Activities

Write-In Student Edition

. . . *to generate energy for today's science learner — you.*

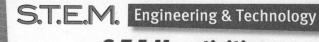

Labs and Activities

ScienceFusion includes lots of exciting hands-on inquiry labs and activities, each one designed to bring science skills and concepts to life and get you involved.

By asking questions, testing your ideas, organizing and analyzing data, drawing conclusions, and sharing what you learn...

You are the scientist!

e-Learning and Virtual Labs

Digital lessons and virtual labs provide e-learning options for every lesson of Science Fusion.

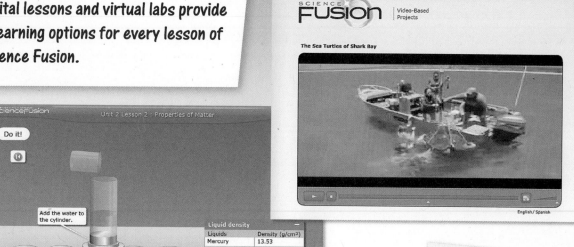

SCIENCE
FUSION | Video-Based Projects

The Sea Turtles of Shark Bay

English / Spanish

Unit 2 Lesson 2 : Properties of Matter

Do it!

Add the water to the cylinder.

Liquid density	
Liquids	Density (g/cm³)
Mercury	13.53
Aniline	1.022
Water	0.998
Paraffin oil	0.88
Mystery liquid	?

mercury   aniline   mystery liquid

On your own or with a group, explore science concepts in a digital world.

360° of Inquiry

Introduction to Waves

Big Idea
Waves transfer energy and interact in predictable ways.

The seven undulating waves of the Henderson Waves Bridge, a pedestrian walkway in Singapore, illustrate some of the properties of waves.

What do you think?

A surfer takes advantage of a wave's energy to catch an exciting ride. What other properties of waves might help a surfer catch a wave?

The higher the ocean wave, the farther the surfer can travel.

Unit 1
Introduction to Waves

Hit the Airwaves

When you hear the word *waves*, you probably think of waves in an ocean. But you encounter waves every day. For example, radio stations use airwaves to broadcast sounds to an audience.

1 Think about It

What do you know about the properties of waves? Sketch and label two full waves in the space below to show your current understanding of waves.

Each number on a radio dial represents a different wave frequency.

② Ask a Question

How does the Federal Communications Commission (FCC) assign the broadcast frequencies for radio and television stations? You might be surprised to discover that the FCC also assigns frequencies for devices that use radio waves. Such devices include garage-door openers and radio-controlled toys. With a partner, research this topic and share your findings with your class.

_____

_____

_____

_____

③ Make a Plan

A Choose a call sign, broadcast frequency (has to be AM), and listening area for a campus radio station based on your research.

_____

_____

_____

B List some other kinds of data you would need to research to start your own campus radio broadcasting station.

_____

_____

_____

_____

C Could you increase the listening area of your radio station?

_____

_____

_____

The airwaves transmit the announcer's voice to listeners far and wide.

Take It Home

Talk with an adult about starting a radio station in your school. What types of programs would students want to hear? Could you actually create a school radio broadcasting station? Write a description of your radio station to turn in to your teacher.

Waves

ESSENTIAL QUESTION

What are waves?

By the end of this lesson, you should be able to distinguish between types of waves based on medium and direction of motion.

Ocean waves can cause great destruction. This woodblock print illustrates a great wave threatening boats off the coast of Japan.

 **Engage Your Brain**

1 Predict Check T or F to show whether you think each statement is true or false.

T   F

☐ ☐ The air around you is full of waves.

☐ ☐ Ocean waves carry water from hundreds of miles away.

☐ ☐ Sound waves can travel across outer space.

☐ ☐ Visible light is a wave.

2 Identify Make a list of items in the classroom that are making waves. Next to each item, write what kind of waves you think it is making.

_____

_____

_____

_____

_____

_____

_____

_____

 Active Reading

3 Distinguish Which of the following definitions of *medium* do you think is most likely to be used in the context of studying waves? Circle your answer.

A of intermediate size

B the matter in which a physical phenomenon takes place

C between two extremes

Vocabulary Terms

• wave
• medium
• longitudinal wave
• transverse wave
• mechanical wave
• electromagnetic wave

4 Apply As you learn the definition of each vocabulary term in this lesson, write your own definition or sketch to help you remember the meaning of the term.

What are waves?

The world is full of waves. Water waves are just one of many kinds of waves. Sound and light are also waves. A **wave** is a disturbance that transfers energy from one place to another.

Waves Are Disturbances

Many waves travel by disturbing a material. The material then returns to its original place. A **medium** is the material through which a wave travels.

You can make waves on a rope by shaking the end up and down. The rope is the medium, and the wave is the up-and-down disturbance. As the part of the rope nearest your hand moves, it causes the part next to it to move up and down too. The motion of this part of the rope causes the next part to move. In this way, the wave moves as a disturbance down the whole length of the rope.

Each piece of the rope moves up and down as a wave goes by. Then the piece of rope returns to where it was before. A wave transfers energy from one place to another. It does not transfer matter. The points where the wave is highest are called crests. The points where the wave is lowest are called troughs.

5 Identify Underline the names for the highest and lowest points of a wave.

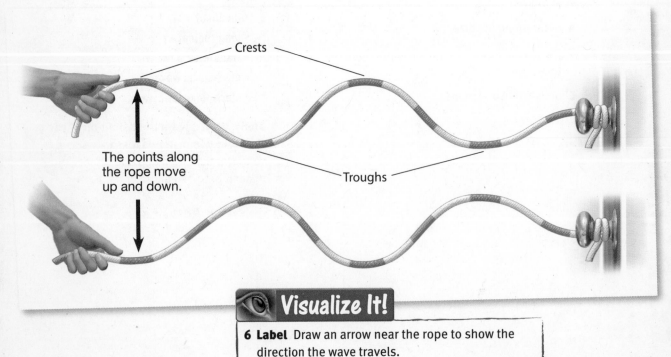

Crests

The points along the rope move up and down.

Troughs

Visualize It!

6 Label Draw an arrow near the rope to show the direction the wave travels.

Waves Are a Transfer of Energy

A wave is a disturbance that transfers energy. Some waves need a medium to transfer energy, such as waves in the ocean that move through water and waves that are carried on guitar or cello strings when they vibrate. Some waves can transfer energy without a medium. One example is visible light. Light waves from the sun transfer energy to Earth across empty space.

Visualize It!

Each snapshot below shows the passage of a wave. The leaf rises and falls as crests and troughs carry it.

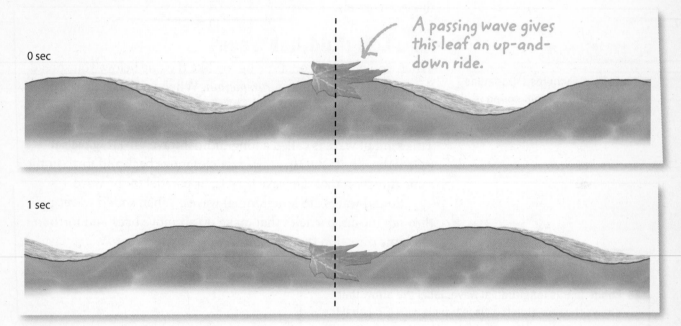

0 sec

A passing wave gives this leaf an up-and-down ride.

1 sec

7 Illustrate In the picture below, draw the leaf in the location it will be after 2 seconds.

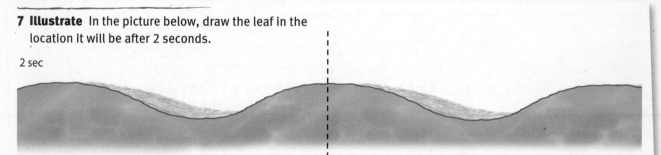

2 sec

8 Model In the space below, draw the leaf and wave as they will appear after 3 seconds.

3 sec

How does a wave transfer energy?

A wave transfers energy in the direction it travels. However, the disturbance may not be in the same direction as the wave. Each wave can be classified by comparing the direction of the disturbance, such as the motion of the medium, with the direction the wave travels.

As a Longitudinal Wave

When you pull back on a spring toy like the one below, you spread the coils apart and make a *rarefaction*. When you push forward, you squeeze the coils closer together and make a *compression*. The coils move back and forth as the wave passes along the spring toy. This kind of wave is called a longitudinal wave. In a **longitudinal wave** (lahn•jih•TOOD•n•uhl), particles move back and forth in the same direction that the wave travels, or parallel to the wave.

Sound waves are longitudinal waves. When sound waves pass through the air, particles that make up air move back and forth in the same direction that the sound waves travel.

> **Active Reading**
>
> **9 Identify** As you read, underline the type of wave that sound is.

> **Visualize It!**
>
> **10 Label** In this longitudinal wave, label the arrow that shows the direction the wave travels with a *T*. Label the arrow that shows how the spring is disturbed with a *D*.

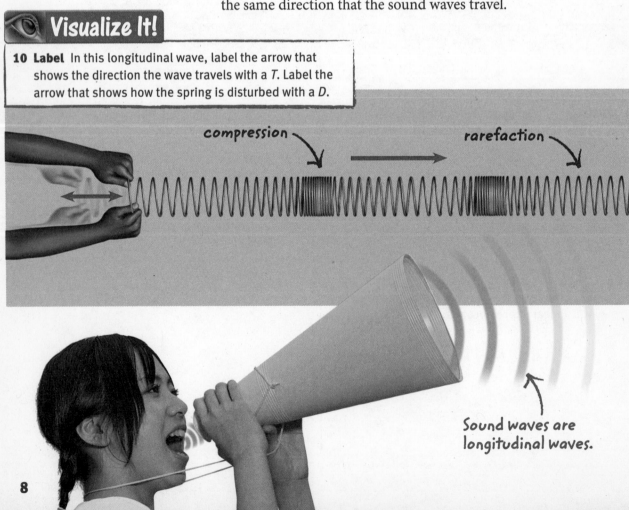

compression

rarefaction

Sound waves are longitudinal waves.

to Transfer Energy

As a Transverse Wave

The same spring toy can be used to make other kinds of waves. If you move the end of the spring toy up and down, a wave also travels along the spring. In this wave, the spring's coils move up and down as the wave passes. This kind of wave is called a **transverse wave**. In a transverse wave, particles move perpendicularly to the direction the wave travels.

Transverse waves and longitudinal waves often travel at different speeds in a medium. In a spring toy, longitudinal waves are usually faster. An earthquake sends both longitudinal waves (called P waves) and transverse waves (called S waves) through Earth's crust. In this case, the longitudinal waves are also faster. During an earthquake, the faster P waves arrive first. A little while later, the S waves arrive. The S waves are slower but usually more destructive.

A transverse wave and a longitudinal wave can combine to form another kind of wave called a surface wave. Ripples on a pond are an example of a surface wave.

When these fans do "The Wave," they are modeling the way a disturbance travels through a medium.

12 Categorize Is the stadium wave shown above a transverse wave or a longitudinal wave?

_____

Think Outside the Book Inquiry

13 Identify What do the letters *S* in S waves and *P* in P waves stand for? Relate this to earthquakes and discuss it with a classmate.

Visualize It!

11 Label In this transverse wave, label the arrow that shows the direction the wave travels with a *T*. Label the arrow that shows how the spring is disturbed with a *D*.

Water waves are surface waves, a combination of transverse and longitudinal waves.

Making Waves

What are some types of waves?

As you have learned, waves are disturbances that transfer energy. Waves can be classified by the direction of disturbance. But they can also be classified by what is disturbed.

Mechanical Waves

Most of the waves we have talked about so far are waves in a medium. For water waves, water is the medium. For earthquake waves, Earth is the medium. A wave that requires a medium through which to travel is called a **mechanical wave**.

Some mechanical waves can travel through more than one medium. For example, sound waves can move through air, through water, or even through a solid wall. The waves travel at different speeds in the different media. Sound waves travel much faster in a liquid or a solid than in air.

Mechanical waves can't travel without a medium. Suppose all the air is removed from beneath a glass dome, or bell jar, as in the photograph below. In a vacuum, there is no air to transmit sound waves. The vibrations made inside the bell jar can't be heard.

Electromagnetic Waves

Are there waves that can travel without a medium? Yes. Sunlight travels from the sun to Earth through empty space. Although light waves can travel through a medium, they can also travel without a medium. Light and similar waves are called electromagnetic (EM) waves. An **electromagnetic wave** is a disturbance in electric and magnetic fields. They are transverse waves. Examples of EM waves include

- visible light
- radio waves
- microwaves
- ultraviolet (UV) light
- x-rays

In empty space, all these waves travel at the same speed. This speed, referred to as the speed of light, is about 300 million meters per second!

The sound from the toy cannot be heard because there is no air to transmit the sound.

Visible light is a type of wave called an electromagnetic wave.

Visualize It!

14 Classify Identify each example of waves in these three photographs as mechanical or electromagnetic.

Sunlight is a(n)
_____

Water waves are
_____

A towel waving displays a(n)
_____

Vocal sounds are
_____

Music is a(n)
_____

Firelight is a(n)
_____

Visual Summary

To complete this summary, fill in the lines below the statement to correct the statement so that it is true. You can use this page to review the main concepts of the lesson.

Waves are disturbances that transfer energy.

15 The water particles in the wave move to the right, along with the wave.

_____
_____
_____

Waves can be longitudinal or transverse.

16 The toy above and the toy below both show longitudinal waves.

_____
_____
_____

Waves

Waves can be mechanical or electromagnetic.

17 This picture shows only examples of mechanical waves.

_____
_____
_____

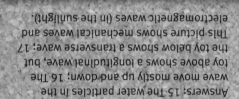

This picture shows mechanical waves and electromagnetic waves (in the sunlight).

18 **Support** Use an example to support the following statement: Waves transfer energy but not matter.

Lesson Review

Vocabulary

Circle the term that best completes the following sentences.

1 A wave is a disturbance that transfers *matter/energy*.

2 In a *longitudinal/transverse* wave, the disturbance moves parallel to the direction the wave travels.

3 *Mechanical/Electromagnetic* waves require a medium in which to travel.

Key Concepts

4–6 Identify Name the medium for each of the following types of waves.

Type of wave	Medium
ocean waves	**4**
earthquake waves	**5**
sound waves from a speaker	**6**

7 Describe Explain how transverse waves can be produced on a rope. Then describe how pieces of the rope move as waves pass.

_____

_____

_____

_____

_____

8 Analyze Are the sun's rays mechanical waves or electromagnetic waves? How do you know?

_____

_____

_____

Critical Thinking

9 Contrast Mechanical waves travel as disturbances in a physical medium. How do electromagnetic waves travel?

_____

_____

_____

Use this image to answer the following questions.

10 Infer Even though the phone is ringing, no sound comes out of the jar. What does this tell you about the space inside the jar?

_____

_____

_____

_____

11 Infer What does this same experiment tell you about light waves? Explain.

_____

_____

_____

_____

_____

My Notes

Mean, Median, Mode, and Range

You can analyze both the measures of central tendency and the variability of data using mean, median, mode, and range.

Tutorial

Imagine that a group of students records the light levels at various places within a classroom.

Classroom Light Levels	
Area	**Illuminance (lux)**
1	800
2	300
3	150
4	300
5	200

Mean The mean is the sum of all of the values in a data set divided by the total number of values in the data set. The mean is also called the *average*.	$$\frac{800 + 300 + 150 + 300 + 200}{5}$$ **mean** = 350 lux
Median The median is the value of the middle item when data are arranged in order by size. In a range that has an odd number of values, the median is the middle value. In a range that has an even number of values, the median is the average of the two middle values.	If necessary, reorder the values from least to greatest: 150, 200, **300**, 300, 800 **median** = 300 lux
Mode The mode is the value or values that occur most frequently in a data set. If all values occur with the same frequency, the data set is said to have no mode. Values should be put in order to find the mode.	If necessary, reorder the values from least to greatest: 150, 200, 300, 300, 800 The value 300 occurs most frequently. **mode** = 300 lux
Range The range is the difference between the greatest value and the least value of a data set.	800 − 150 **range** = 650 lux

You Try It!

The data table below shows the data collected for rooms in three halls in the school.

Illuminance (lux)				
	Room 1	Room 2	Room 3	Room 4
Science Hall	150	250	500	400
Art Hall	300	275	550	350
Math Hall	200	225	600	600

Using Formulas Find the mean, median, mode, and range of the data for the school.

Analyzing Methods The school board is looking into complaints that some areas of the school are too poorly lit. They are considering replacing the lights. If you were in favor of replacing the lights, which representative value for the school's data would you use to support your position? If you were opposed to replacing the lights, which representative value for the school's data would you choose to support your position? Explain your answer.

_____

_____

_____

_____

_____

_____

_____

_____

_____

_____

_____

Language Arts Connection

On flashcards, write sentences that use the keywords *mean, median, mode,* and *range*. Cover the keywords with small sticky notes. Review each sentence, and determine if it provides enough context clues to determine the covered word. If necessary, work with a partner to improve your sentences.

Properties of Waves

ESSENTIAL QUESTION

How can we describe a wave?

By the end of this lesson, you should be able to identify characteristics of a wave and describe wave behavior.

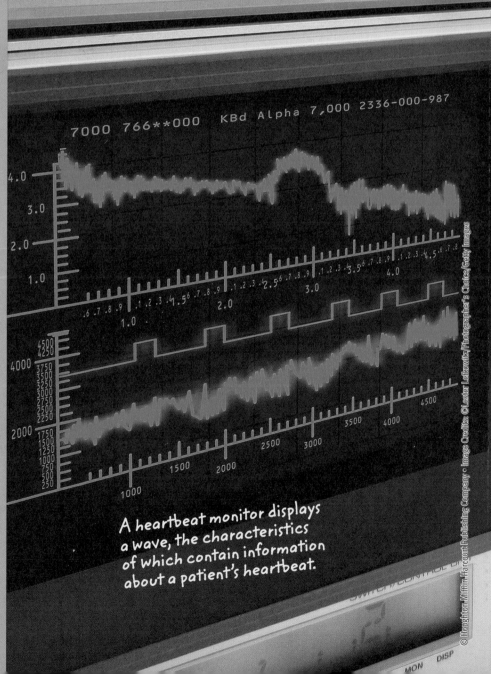

A heartbeat monitor displays a wave, the characteristics of which contain information about a patient's heartbeat.

Lesson Labs

Quick Labs
- Investigate Frequency
- Waves on a Spring

Exploration Lab
- Investigate Wavelength

Engage Your Brain

1 Describe Fill in the blank with the word that you think correctly completes the following sentences.

A guitar amplifier makes a guitar sound

_____

FM radio frequencies are measured in mega- _____

The farther you are from a sound source, the _____ the sound is.

2 Illustrate Draw a diagram of a wave in the space below. How would you describe your wave so that a friend on the phone could duplicate your drawing?

Active Reading

3 Predict Many scientific words also have everyday meanings. For each of the following terms, write in your own words what it means in common use. Then try writing a definition of what it might mean when applied to waves.

length:

_____
_____
_____
_____
_____

speed:

_____
_____
_____
_____

period (of time):

_____
_____
_____

Vocabulary Terms

- **wave**
- **amplitude**
- **wavelength**
- **wave period**
- **frequency**
- **hertz**
- **wave speed**

4 Compare This list contains the vocabulary terms you'll learn in this lesson. As you read, circle the definition of each term.

Amp It UP!

How can we describe a wave?

Suppose you are talking to a friend who had been to the beach. You want to know what the waves were like. Were they big or small? How often did they come? How far apart were they? Were they moving fast? Each of these is a basic property that can be used to describe waves.

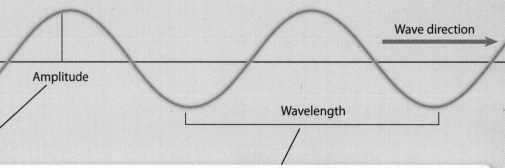

Wave direction

Amplitude

Wavelength

By Its Amplitude

A **wave** is a disturbance that transfers energy from one place to another. As a wave passes, particles in the medium move up and down or back and forth. A wave's **amplitude** is a measure of how far the particles in the medium move away from their normal rest position. The graph above shows a transverse wave. Notice that the amplitude of a wave is also half of the difference between the highest and lowest values.

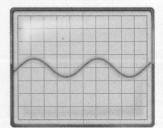 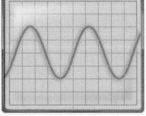

By Its Wavelength

You can use amplitude to describe the height of an ocean wave, for example. But to describe how long the wave is, you need to know its wavelength. The **wavelength** is the distance from any point on a wave to an identical point on the next wave. For example, wavelength is the distance from one crest to the next, from one trough to the next, or between any other two corresponding points. Wavelength measures the length of one cycle, or repetition.

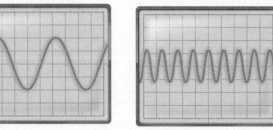 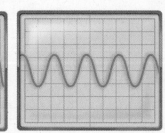

👁 **Visualize It!**

5 Label Mark the amplitude in the two graphs above. Which wave has the greater amplitude?

_____

6 Label Mark the wavelength in the two graphs above. Which wave has the greater wavelength?

_____

By Its Frequency

Wavelength and amplitude tell you about the size of a wave. Another property tells you how much time a wave takes to repeat. The **wave period** (usually "period") is the time required for one cycle. You can measure the period by finding the time for one full cycle of a wave to pass a given point. For example, you could start timing when one crest passes you and stop when the next crest passes. The time between two crests is the period.

Another way to express the time of a wave's cycle is frequency. The **frequency** of a wave tells how many cycles occur in an amount of time, usually 1 s. Frequency is expressed in **hertz** (Hz). One hertz is equal to one cycle per second. If ten crests pass each second, the frequency is 10 Hz.

> Frequency and period are closely related. Frequency is the inverse of period:
>
> $$\text{frequency} = \frac{1}{\text{period}}$$

Suppose the time from one crest to another—the period—is 5 s. The frequency is then $\frac{1}{5}$ Hz, or 0.2 Hz. In other words, one-fifth (0.2) of a wave passes each second.

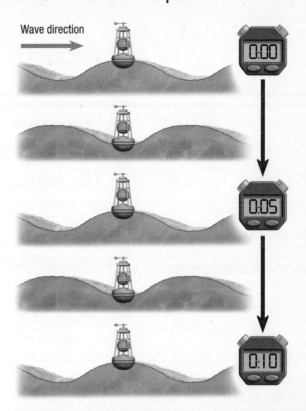

The buoy moves down and back up every five seconds as waves pass.

Wave direction

> Frequency is equal to the number of cycles per unit of time:
>
> $$\text{frequency} = \frac{\text{number of cycles}}{\text{time}}$$

Visualize It!

7 Illustrate On the grid below, draw a wave, and then draw another wave with twice the amplitude.

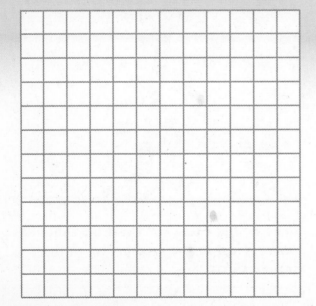

8 Illustrate On the grid below, draw a wave, and then draw another wave with half the wavelength.

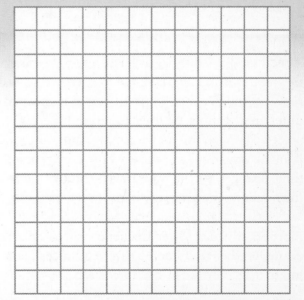

Amp It Down

What affects the energy of a wave?

All waves carry energy from one place to another, but some waves carry more energy than others. A leaf falling on water produces waves so small they are hard to see. An earthquake under the ocean can produce huge waves that cause great destruction.

The Amplitude or The Frequency

For a mechanical wave, amplitude is related to the amount of energy the wave carries. For two similar waves, the wave with greater amplitude carries more energy. For example, sound waves with greater amplitude transfer more energy to your eardrum, so they sound louder.

Greater frequency can also mean greater energy in a given amount of time. If waves hit a barrier three times in a minute, they transfer a certain amount of energy to the barrier. If waves of the same amplitude hit nine times in a minute, they transfer more energy in that minute.

For most electromagnetic (EM) waves, energy is most strongly related to frequency. Very high-frequency EM waves, such as x-rays and gamma rays, carry enough energy to damage human tissue. Lower-frequency EM waves, such as visible light waves, can be absorbed safely by your body.

Active Reading

9 Identify As you read, underline the kind of wave whose energy depends mostly on frequency.

Think Outside the Book

10 Apply An echo is the reflection of sound waves as they bounce back after hitting a barrier. How can the design of a building, such as a concert hall, reduce unwanted noises and echoes?

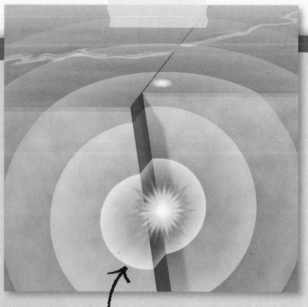

Some of the energy of these earthquake waves is lost to the medium when the ground shifts.

Energy Loss to a Medium

A medium transmits a wave. However, a medium may not transmit all of the wave's energy. As a wave moves through a medium, particles may move in different directions or come to rest in different places. The medium may warm up, shift, or change in other ways. Some of the wave's energy produces these changes. As the wave travels through more of the medium, more energy is lost to the medium.

Often, higher-frequency waves lose energy more readily than lower-frequency waves. For example, when you stand far from a concert, you might hear only the low-frequency (bass) sounds.

Energy Loss Due to Spreading

So far, we have mostly talked about waves moving in straight lines. But waves usually spread out in more than one dimension. The crests can be drawn as shapes, such as circles or spheres, called *wavefronts*. As each wavefront moves farther from the source, the energy is spread over a greater area. Less energy is available at any one point on the wavefront. If you measure a wave at a point farther from the source, you measure less energy. But the total energy of the wavefront stays the same.

Sound waves expand in three dimensions.

Ripples on a water surface expand in two dimensions.

Inquiry

11 Predict Which type of wave spreading do you think causes faster energy loss—two-dimensional or three-dimensional? Explain.

_____

_____

_____

As the student on the left knocks on the table, the students farther away feel the resulting waves less strongly.

Visualize It! Inquiry

12 Synthesize If these students repeated their experiment using a longer table, what differences would they observe? Explain your answer.

_____

_____

_____

A Happy Medium

What determines the speed of a wave?

Waves travel at different speeds in different media. For example, sound waves travel at about 340 m/s in air at room temperature, but they travel at nearly 1,500 m/s in water. In a solid, sound waves travel even faster.

The Medium in Which It Travels

The speed at which a wave travels—called **wave speed**—depends on the properties of the medium. Specifically, wave speed depends on the interactions of the atomic particles of the medium. In general, waves travel faster in solids than in liquids and faster in liquids than in gases. Interactions, or collisions, between particles happen faster in solids because the particles are close together.

How fast the wave travels between particles within the medium depends on many factors. For example, wave speed depends on the density of the medium. Waves usually travel slower in the denser of two solids or the denser of two liquids. The more densely packed the particles are, the more they resist motion, so they transfer waves more slowly.

In a gas, wave speed depends on temperature as well as density. Particles in hot air move faster than particles in cold air, so particles in hot air collide more often. This faster interaction allows waves to pass through hot air more quickly than through cold air, even though hot air may be less dense. The speed of sound in air at 20 °C is about 340 m/s. The speed of sound in air at 0 °C is slower, about 330 m/s.

Electromagnetic waves don't require a medium, so they can travel in a vacuum. All electromagnetic waves travel at the same speed in empty space. This speed, called the speed of light, is about 300,000,000 m/s. While passing through a medium such as air or glass, EM waves travel more slowly than they do in a vacuum.

Active Reading **13 Identify** Does sound travel faster or slower when the air gets warmer?

Visualize It!

14 Diagram One diagram shows sound traveling through an air-filled tank. Draw a medium in the second tank in which sound will travel faster than in the air-filled tank.

Air

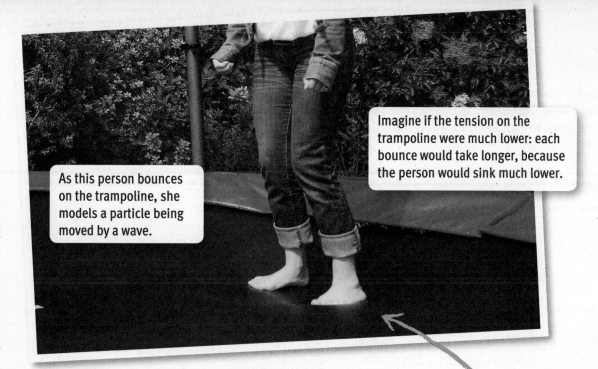

As this person bounces on the trampoline, she models a particle being moved by a wave.

Imagine if the tension on the trampoline were much lower: each bounce would take longer, because the person would sink much lower.

Its Frequency and Wavelength

Wave speed can be calculated from frequency and wavelength. To understand how, it helps to remember that speed is defined as distance divided by time:

As a medium becomes more flexible, it carries waves more slowly.

$$speed = \frac{distance}{time}$$

So if a runner runs 8 m in 2 s, then the runner's speed is 8 m ÷ 2 s = 4 m/s. For a wave, a crest moves a distance of one wavelength in one cycle. The time for the cycle to occur is one period. Using wavelength and period as the distance and time:

$$wave\ speed = \frac{wavelength}{wave\ period}$$

So if a crest moves one wavelength of 8 m in one period of 2 s, the wave speed is calculated just like the runner's speed: 8 m ÷ 2 s = 4 m/s.

Frequency is the inverse of the wave period. So the relationship can be rewritten like this:

$$wave\ speed = frequency \times wavelength$$
$$or$$
$$wavelength = \frac{wave\ speed}{frequency}$$

If you already know the wave speed, you can use this equation to solve for frequency or wavelength.

 **Do the Math** **You Try It**

15 Calculate Complete this table relating wave speed, frequency, and wavelength.

Wave speed (m/s)	Frequency (Hz)	Wavelength (m)
20		5
75	15	
	23	16
625		25
	38	20

Visual Summary

To complete this summary, fill in the blanks with the correct word or phrase. Then use the key below to check your answers. You can use this page to review the main concepts of the lesson.

Amplitude tells the amount of displacement of a wave.

Wavelength tells how long a wave is.

Wave period is the time required for one cycle.

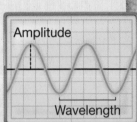

Amplitude

Wavelength

16 _____ $= \dfrac{1}{\text{wave period}}$

17 Hertz is used to express _____

18 One hertz is equal to _____

Wave energy depends on amplitude and frequency.

Most waves lose energy over time as they travel and spread.

20 Some of the wave's energy stays in the _____

Wave Properties

Wave speed depends on the properties of the medium.

In a vacuum, electromagnetic waves all move at the speed of light.

19 wave speed = frequency × _____

Answers: 16 frequency; 17 frequency; 18 one cycle per second; 19 wavelength; 20 medium

21 **Synthesize** Describe how the properties of sound waves change as they spread out in a spherical pattern.

Lesson Review

Vocabulary

Fill in the blank with the correct letter.

1 frequency

_____

2 wavelength

_____

3 wave speed

_____

4 wave period

_____

5 amplitude

_____

A the distance over which a wave's shape repeats

B the maximum distance that particles in a wave's medium vibrate from their rest position

C the time required for one wavelength to pass a point

D the number of wavelengths that pass a point in a given amount of time

E the speed at which a wave travels through a medium

Key Concepts

6 Describe What measures the amount of displacement in a transverse wave?

_____

7 Relate How are frequency and wave period related?

_____

_____

_____

_____

8 Provide What does the energy of an electromagnetic wave depend on?

_____

9 Infer Sound travels slower in colder air than it does in warmer air. Why does the speed of sound depend on air temperature?

_____

_____

_____

_____

_____

_____

Critical Thinking

Use this diagram to answer the following questions. The frequency of the wave is 0.5 Hz.

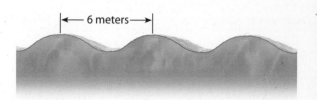

←— 6 meters —→

10 Analyze What is the wavelength of these waves?

_____

11 Calculate What is the speed of these waves?

_____

12 Solve If you were sitting in a boat as these waves passed by, how many seconds would pass between wave crests?

_____

13 Infer Why does the energy of a sound wave decrease over time?

_____

_____

_____

14 Infer A wave has a low speed but a high frequency. What can you infer about its wavelength?

_____

_____

15 Predict How do you know the speed of an electromagnetic wave in a vacuum?

_____

_____

_____

_____

My Notes

Lesson 1

ESSENTIAL QUESTION
What are waves?

Distinguish between
types of waves based
on medium and
direction of motion.

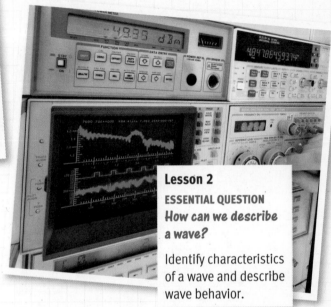

Lesson 2

ESSENTIAL QUESTION
*How can we describe
a wave?*

Identify characteristics
of a wave and describe
wave behavior.

Connect ESSENTIAL QUESTIONS
Lessons 1 and 2

1 Synthesize What are two properties of waves
that affect the energy of waves?

_____

_____

Think Outside the Book

2 Synthesize Choose one of these activities
to help synthesize what you have learned in
this unit.

☐ Using what you learned in lessons 1 and 2,
create a model that compares the parts
of a mechanical wave to the parts of an
electromagnetic wave.

☐ Using what you learned in lessons 1 and
2, design an experiment to compare
mechanical wave speeds through different
media. Include all of the steps in your
process and provide illustrations where
needed.

Unit 1 Review

Name _____

Vocabulary

Fill in each blank with the term that best completes the following sentences.

1 Light travels as a(n) _____ wave.

2 The distance from the crest of one wave to the crest of the next wave is
the _____

3 _____, the number of waves produced in a given
amount of time, is expressed in hertz.

4 Sound is a(n) _____ wave because it cannot travel
without a medium.

5 The maximum distance that the particles of a medium move away from their rest
position is a measure of a wave's _____

Key Concepts

Read each question below, and circle the best answer.

6 Sashita uses the volume control on her TV to make the sound louder or softer.
Which property of waves is Sashita's volume control changing?

A amplitude

B wave period

C wavelength

D wave speed

7 Which statement best explains what waves are?

A wavy lines on graph paper

B disturbances that transfer energy

C light energy that changes into particles of matter

D circles that move out from a central place

8 The diagram below shows the properties of a transverse wave.

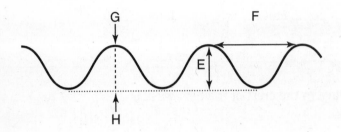

What property of the wave does F measure?

A period

C amplitude

B frequency

D wavelength

9 Which type of electromagnetic waves have the highest frequency?

A radio waves

C light waves

B gamma rays

D x-rays

10 Isabella researched how waves travel through the ground during an earthquake. She drew a diagram of one, called an S wave, moving through Earth's crust.

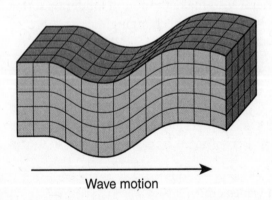

Wave motion

Based on her diagram, what kind of wave is an S wave?

A light

B sound

C longitudinal

D transverse

11 Visible, infrared, and ultraviolet light are electromagnetic waves that travel from the sun to Earth. The diagram below shows some types of electromagnetic waves.

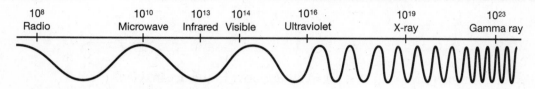

The Electromagnetic Spectrum
Typical frequency in hertz (1 hertz = 1 wavelength/second)

Which statement best explains what electromagnetic waves are?

A waves that vibrate through a medium

B disturbances in the atmosphere of space

C disturbances in electric and magnetic fields

D slow-moving waves

12 Frequency equals the number of wavelengths per unit of time.

$$\text{Frequency} = \frac{\text{Wavelengths}}{\text{Unit of time}}$$

Which unit is used to measure frequency as cycles per second?

A hertz

C crest

B period

D minute

13 Which statement about the effects of medium on the speed of a mechanical wave is true?

A Medium has no effect on the speed of a mechanical wave.

B A mechanical wave generally travels faster in solids than liquids.

C A mechanical wave generally travels faster in gases than liquids.

D A mechanical wave always travels through liquids at the speed of light.

Critical Thinking

Answer the following questions in the space provided.

14 Some waves carry more energy than others. Which wave has more energy, a loud sound or a quiet sound? Why?

_____

_____

15 Tafari worked one summer on a ship that set weather buoys in the ocean. He watched how the buoys moved in the water.

Which wave property describes why the buoys bobbed up and down?

Which wave property determines how fast the buoys bobbed in the water?

He observed that when the wind blew harder, the ocean waves were larger, and the buoys moved away from the ship. What effect, if any, did the waves have on how far the buoys moved? Explain your answer.

_____

_____

_____

_____

Connect **ESSENTIAL QUESTIONS**
Lessons 1 and 2

Answer the following question in the space provided.

16 Jung arrived at a concert in the park so late that the only seat she could get was almost a block from the stage. The music sounded much fainter to Jung than it did to people near the stage. She could hear the drums and bass guitar fairly well, but she had trouble hearing higher sounds from the singer. Explain the properties and behavior of waves that affected how Jung heard the music.

_____

_____

_____

_____

_____

Sound

Big Idea
Sound waves transfer energy through vibrations.

The Singing Ringing Tree, located in rural England, enchants visitors with an eerie hum. The sound is created by the wind passing through the galvanized steel pipes.

What do you think?

Music is just one example of sound. Describe some sounds you heard today. Are these sounds produced by human activity or by nature?

The clarinetist uses "wind" to make music.

CITIZEN SCIENCE

Sound It Out!

Have you ever felt a vibrating sensation during a really loud sound? That happens because sound waves transfer energy in the form of vibrations. You can learn how to make sounds louder and quieter by investigating sound sculptures.

1 Do Additional Research

Investigate the Singing Ringing Tree by finding a book about it in the library or doing an Internet search. How does the sculpture produce sound?

_____

_____

_____

_____

_____

_____

The cheerleader uses a megaphone to make her voice louder.

② Think about It

What would make the sound louder?
What would make the sound quieter?
Write your ideas below.

Louder	Quieter

A mute is used to make the trumpet quieter.

③ Make A Plan

A You can make your own sound sculpture with everyday objects. Think about how you would create sound with some of the following items: spoons, drinking straws, plastic bottles, pencils, paper clips, sheets of paper, cellophane, rubber bands, or plastic cups. Will wind be the source of your sound? Write a prediction about how it will sound.

_____

_____

_____

_____

_____

B Sketch your sculpture in the space below.

ear trumpet

Take It Home

With an adult, research devices used by people who were hard of hearing in 1900, in 1960, and today. Over the years, how have these devices changed or stayed the same?

Lesson 1

Sound Waves and Hearing

ESSENTIAL QUESTION

What is sound?

By the end of this lesson, you should be able to describe what sound is, identify its properties, and explain how humans hear it.

Musical instruments produce sound by making vibrations.

Lesson Labs

Quick Labs
• Investigate Sound Energy
• Different Instrument Sounds
• Investigate Loudness

Exploration Lab
• Sound Idea

Engage Your Brain

1 Predict Check T or F to show whether you think each sentence below about sound is correct.

T	F	
☐	☐	Sound reaches our ears as waves.
☐	☐	Loud sounds are not harmful to humans.
☐	☐	All animals hear the same range of frequencies.
☐	☐	Sound can travel in outer space.
☐	☐	Sound can travel in water.

2 Describe Why is this woman wearing ear protection? Write your answer in the form of a caption for this photograph.

_____

_____

_____

Active Reading

3 Apply Use context clues to write your own definition for the term *longitudinal wave*.

Example sentence:
The <u>longitudinal wave</u> traveled back and forth along the length of the coiled spring.

longitudinal wave:

_____

_____

_____

_____

Vocabulary Terms

• sound wave   • loudness
• longitudinal wave   • decibel
• pitch   • Doppler effect

4 Identify As you read, create a reference card for each vocabulary term. On one side of the card, write the term and its meaning. On the other side, draw an image that illustrates or makes a connection to the term. Use your cards as bookmarks in the text so that you can refer to them while studying.

Listen Up!

What is sound?

When you beat a drum, the drum skin vibrates and causes the air to vibrate, as shown below. A *vibration* is the complete back-and-forth motion of an object. The vibrations in the air are interpreted as sounds by your brain. No matter how different they are, all sounds are created by vibrations.

What are sound waves?

A **sound wave** is a longitudinal wave that is caused by vibrations and travels through a medium. In a **longitudinal wave** the particles of a medium vibrate in the same direction that the wave travels. Longitudinal waves, also called *compression waves,* are made of compressions and rarefactions (rair•uh•FAK•shuhns). A *compression* is the part of a longitudinal wave where particles are close together. A *rarefaction* is the part where particles are spread apart. As the wave passes through a medium, its particles are compressed together and then spread apart.

Active Reading

5 Identify As you read, underline the properties of longitudinal waves.

Visualize It!

6 Label Write labels for A and B on the sound wave in the diagram.

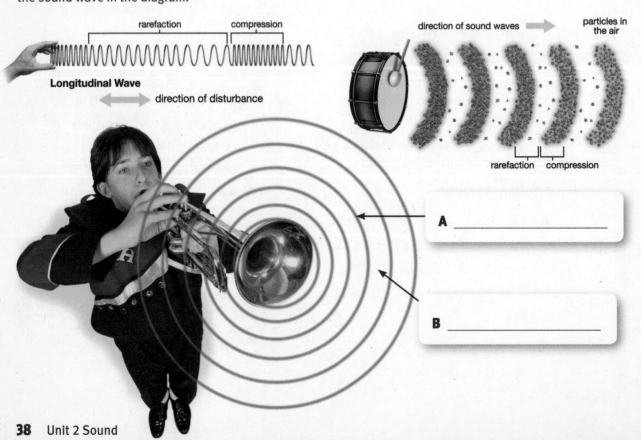

rarefaction   compression

Longitudinal Wave

direction of disturbance

direction of sound waves   particles in the air

rarefaction   compression

A _____

B _____

How do sound waves travel?

Sound waves travel in all directions away from their source, as shown in the photo of the student playing the trumpet. But this is only possible if there is a medium through which the sound waves can travel.

Through a Medium

All matter—solids, liquids, and gases—is composed of particles. Sound waves travel by disturbing the particles in matter, or a medium. The particles of the medium do not travel with the sound waves themselves. The particles of a medium only vibrate back and forth along the path that the sound wave travels.

Most of the sounds that you hear travel through air at least part of the time. Sound waves can also travel through other materials, such as water, glass, and metal. You have probably heard people talking or dogs barking on the other side of a window or door. When you swim underwater, you may hear the sounds of your swim buddies as they splash and call to each other above the surface.

In a vacuum, there are no particles to vibrate. Therefore, no sound can be made in a vacuum. This fact helps to explain the effect shown in the photograph below. Sound must travel through air or some other medium to reach your ears and be detected.

Active Reading 7 **Explain** Why can't sound travel through a vacuum?

_____

_____

_____

_____

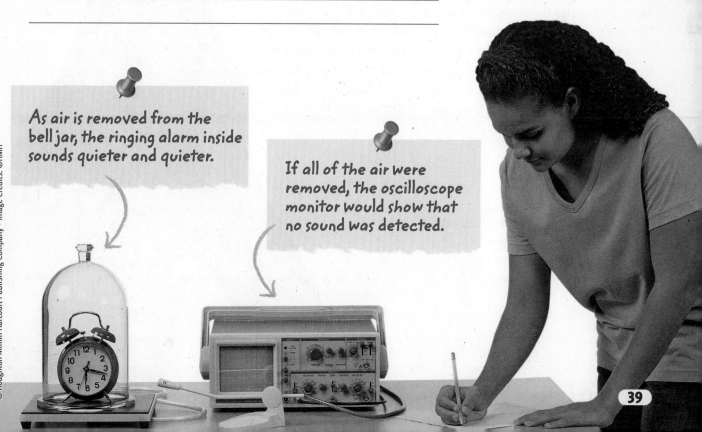

As air is removed from the bell jar, the ringing alarm inside sounds quieter and quieter.

If all of the air were removed, the oscilloscope monitor would show that no sound was detected.

Do You *Hear* That?

How do humans hear sound?

Humans detect sound with their ears. The ear acts like a funnel for sound waves. The ear directs sound vibrations from the environment into the inner ear, where the vibrations are converted to electrical signals. The electrical signals are sent to the brain, which interprets them as sound.

Humans Hear Sound Through Ears

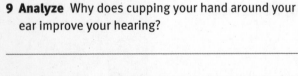 **8 Match** As you read, match each paragraph to the numbered part of the ear illustration on the facing page.

_____ Sound from the environment enters the outer ear, travels through the ear canal, and reaches the eardrum. The eardrum is a thin membrane that is stretched tightly over the entrance to the middle ear. The compressions and rarefactions in the sound waves make the eardrum vibrate.

_____ The eardrum transfers the vibrations to three tiny, connected bones in the middle ear. These bones are called the hammer, anvil, and stirrup. The bones carry vibrations from the eardrum to the oval window, which is the entrance to the inner ear.

_____ The vibrations pass through the oval window and travel through the fluid in the snail-shaped cochlea (KAHK•lee•uh). The cochlea has thousands of nerve cells, and each nerve cell has thousands of tiny surface hairs. The vibrations of the sound waves cause the cochlea fluid to move. The movement of the fluid bends the tiny hairs. The bending hairs make the nerve cells send electrical signals to the brain through the auditory nerve. The brain receives these electrical signals; then it interprets them as the sound that you hear.

The ear is the organ that detects sound.

9 Analyze Why does cupping your hand around your ear improve your hearing?

_____

_____

_____

_____

The Human Ear

The human ear has many parts that all work together to capture and interpret sound waves.

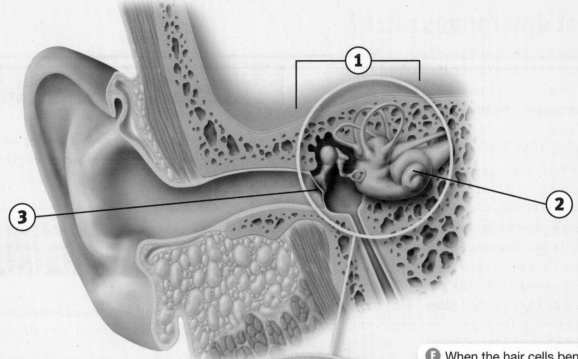

F When the hair cells bend, they stimulate the auditory nerve. The nerve sends electrical signals to the brain, which interprets them as the sounds we hear.

A Sound waves vibrate the eardrum—a tightly stretched membrane that forms the entrance to the middle ear.

E Movement of the liquid causes tiny hair cells inside the cochlea to bend.

B The eardrum vibrates, causing the hammer to vibrate. This in turn makes the anvil and the stirrup vibrate.

D The vibrations of the oval window create waves in the liquid inside the cochlea.

C The stirrup vibrates the oval window—the entrance to the inner ear.

10 Predict If the nerve cells inside the cochlea were damaged, how might hearing be affected?

_____

_____

_____

Can You Hear Me NOW?

What determines pitch?

Pitch is how high or low you think a sound is. The pitch you hear depends on the ear's sensitivity to pitches over a wide range. Pitch depends on the frequency and wavelength of a sound wave.

Frequency and Wavelength

Frequency is expressed in hertz (Hz). One hertz is one complete wavelength, or cycle, per second. In a given medium, the higher the frequency of a wave, the shorter its wavelength and the higher its pitch. High-frequency waves have shorter wavelengths and produce high-pitched sounds. A low-frequency wave has a longer wavelength and makes a low-pitched sound. The diagrams at right show how frequency, wavelength, and pitch are related.

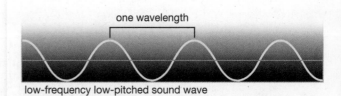

one wavelength

low-frequency low-pitched sound wave

A low-pitched sound has sound waves with a low frequency and a longer wavelength.

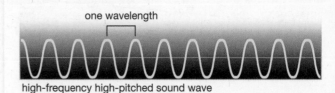

one wavelength

high-frequency high-pitched sound wave

A high-pitched sound has sound waves with a high frequency and a shorter wavelength.

Approximate Sound Frequencies Heard by Animals

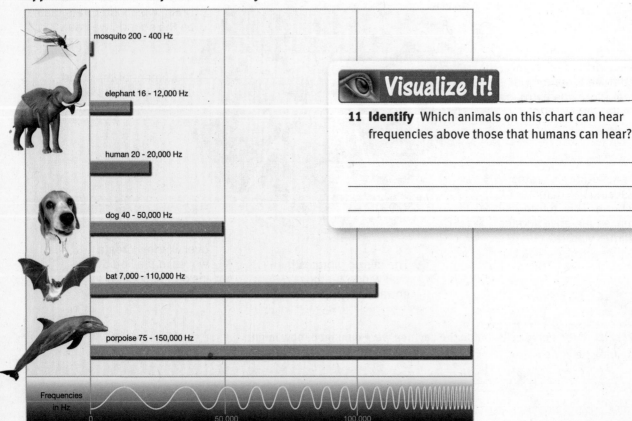

mosquito 200 - 400 Hz

elephant 16 - 12,000 Hz

human 20 - 20,000 Hz

dog 40 - 50,000 Hz

bat 7,000 - 110,000 Hz

porpoise 75 - 150,000 Hz

Frequencies in Hz

0   50,000   100,000

Visualize It!

11 Identify Which animals on this chart can hear frequencies above those that humans can hear?

_____

_____

_____

What makes a sound loud?

If you gently tap a drum, you will hear a soft rumbling. But if you strike the drum much harder, with more force, you will hear a much louder sound. By changing the force you use to strike the drum, you change the loudness of the sound it makes. **Loudness** is a measure of how well a sound can be heard.

Amplitude

The measure of how much energy a sound wave carries is the wave's intensity, or amplitude. The *amplitude* of a sound wave is the maximum distance that the particles of a wave's medium vibrate from their rest position. When you strike a drum harder, you increase the amplitude of the sound waves. The greater the amplitude, the louder the sound; the smaller the amplitude, the softer the sound.

One way to increase loudness is with an amplifier, as shown below. An amplifier receives sound signals in the form of electric current. The amplifier increases the sound wave's energy by increasing the wave's amplitude, which makes the sound louder.

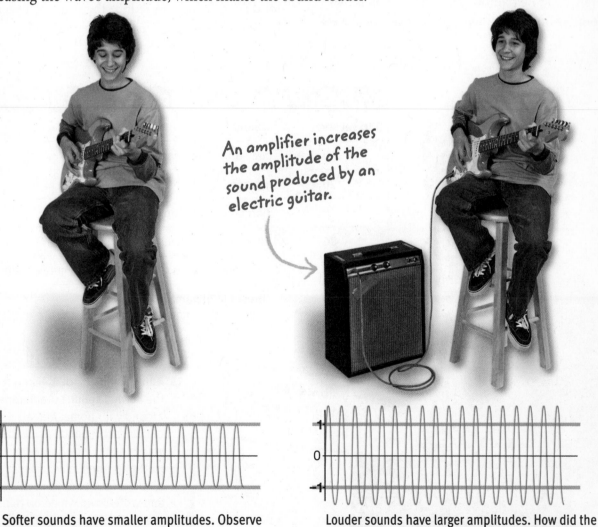

An amplifier increases the amplitude of the sound produced by an electric guitar.

Softer sounds have smaller amplitudes. Observe that the amplitude is 0 to 1, or 0 to −1.

Louder sounds have larger amplitudes. How did the amplitude change? Did the frequency change?

Active Reading

12 Explain What is the relationship between amplitude and the loudness of a sound?

_____

_____

_____

Turn That DOWN!

How is loudness measured?

Loudness is a characteristic of sound that can be calculated from the intensity of a sound wave. The most common unit used to express loudness is the **decibel** (DES•uh•bel). One decibel (dB) is one-tenth of a *bel,* the base unit, although the bel is rarely used. The bel is named after Alexander Graham Bell, who is credited with inventing the telephone.

The softest sounds most humans can hear are at a level of 0 dB. Sounds that are 120 dB or higher can be painful. The table below shows some common sounds and their decibel levels.

How loud is too loud?

Short exposures to sounds that are loud enough to be painful can cause hearing loss. Even loud sounds that are not painful can damage your hearing if you are exposed to them for long periods. Loud sounds can damage the hairs on the nerve cells in the cochlea. Once these hairs are damaged, they do not grow back.

There are simple ways to protect your hearing. Use earplugs to block loud sounds. Lower the volume when using earbuds, and move away from a speaker that is playing loud music. If you double the distance between yourself and a loud sound, you can reduce the sound's intensity by as much as one-fourth of what it was.

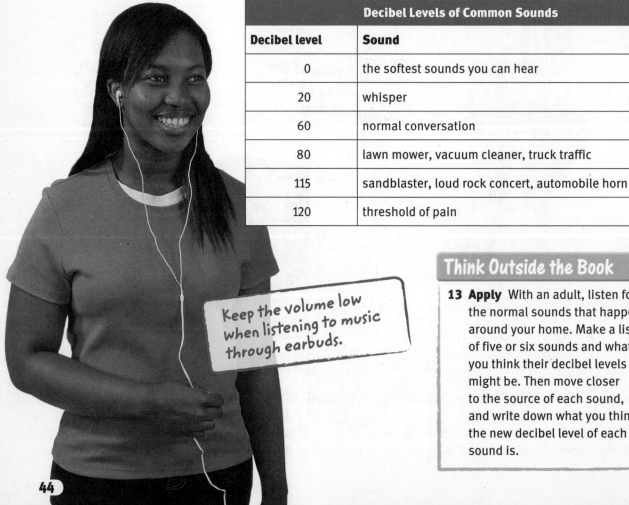

Decibel Levels of Common Sounds	
Decibel level	Sound
0	the softest sounds you can hear
20	whisper
60	normal conversation
80	lawn mower, vacuum cleaner, truck traffic
115	sandblaster, loud rock concert, automobile horn
120	threshold of pain

Keep the volume low when listening to music through earbuds.

Think Outside the Book

13 Apply With an adult, listen for the normal sounds that happen around your home. Make a list of five or six sounds and what you think their decibel levels might be. Then move closer to the source of each sound, and write down what you think the new decibel level of each sound is.

What is the Doppler effect?

Have you ever been stopped at a railroad crossing when a train with its whistle blowing went past? You probably noticed the sudden change in the pitch of the whistle as the train passed. This change in pitch is called the Doppler effect (DAHP•ler ih•FEKT). The **Doppler effect** is a change in the observed frequency of a wave when the sound source, the observer, or both are moving.

As shown in the diagram below, when you and the source of the sound are moving closer together, the sound waves are closer together. The sound has a higher frequency and a higher pitch. When you and the source are moving away from each other, the waves are farther apart. The sound has a lower frequency and a lower pitch.

Active Reading

14 Identify As you read, underline the main points that explain the Doppler effect.

Visualize It!

15 Label In the diagram below, consider the sound waves heard by the people as the train passes them. Label the sound wave that has a higher pitch and the sound wave that has a lower pitch.

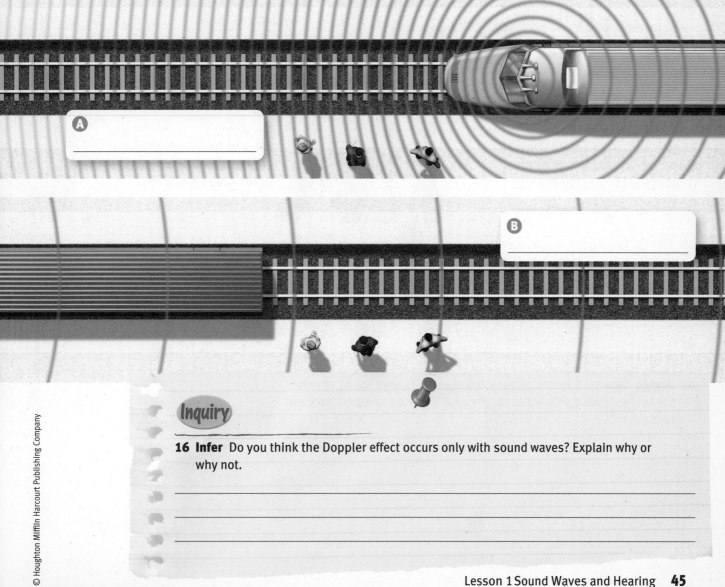

A

B

Inquiry

16 Infer Do you think the Doppler effect occurs only with sound waves? Explain why or why not.

_____

_____

_____

Visual Summary

To complete this summary, fill in the blanks with the correct word or phrase. Then, use the key below to check your answers. You can use this page to review the main concepts of the lesson.

Sound waves are longitudinal waves that cause particles to vibrate.

17 Sound waves must travel through a

_____

Sound Waves and Hearing

The Doppler effect is the change in pitch you hear when the source of a wave, the observer, or both are moving.

18 As a train approaches, the pitch of its whistle sounds

_____

Human ears hear sound when vibrations of sound waves are transmitted to the brain as electrical signals.

Pitch is how high or low a sound is, while amplitude determines loudness.

19 The surface of the nerve cells in the cochlea contain thousands of

_____

20 As the amplitude of a sound increases, the sound becomes _____

Answers: 17 medium; 18 higher; 19 tiny hair cells; 20 louder

21 **Design** Develop a simple demonstration using a coiled spring to model the following wave properties: longitudinal vibration, compression, and rarefaction.

Lesson Review

Vocabulary

Define Fill in the blank with the term that best completes the following sentences.

1 A _____ is an example of a longitudinal wave.

2 _____ is how high or low you think a sound is.

3 Loudness is expressed in _____

Key Concepts

4 **Explain** Describe the properties of a longitudinal wave.

_____

_____

_____

_____

5 **Sequence** Describe how the human ear hears sound.

_____

_____

_____

_____

_____

6 **Explain** How are frequency, wavelength and pitch related?

_____

_____

_____

7 **Summarize** How does amplitude determine loudness?

_____

_____

_____

_____

Critical Thinking

Use the illustration to answer the following questions.

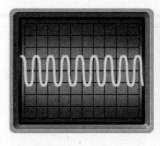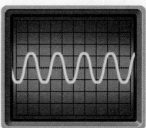

8 **Analyze** The screens show two sound waves that last the same amount of time. Which wave has a higher frequency? Explain your answer.

_____

_____

_____

_____

9 **Analyze** Suppose these waves represent the sound of a siren on a passing ambulance. Which wave represents the sound of the siren *after* it has passed you? Explain your answer.

_____

_____

_____

_____

_____

10 **Analyze** If a meteorite crashed onto the moon, would you be able hear it on Earth? Why or why not?

_____

_____

_____

11 **Apply** Is it safe to listen to music at a level of 115 decibels? Explain why or why not.

_____

_____

_____

My Notes

Interactions of Sound Waves

ESSENTIAL QUESTION

How do sound waves travel and interact?

By the end of this lesson, you should be able to describe how sound waves interact, and how they can cause echoes and sonic booms.

Bats are one type of animal that uses sound waves to avoid obstacles and to find food.

Lesson Labs

Quick Labs
• Resonance in a Bottle
• The Speed of Sound

S.T.E.M. Lab
• Echoes

Engage Your Brain

1 Predict Check T or F to show whether you think each statement is true or false.

T F

☐ ☐ Humans can hear sounds at any frequency.

☐ ☐ Sound waves can combine to become bigger or smaller.

☐ ☐ It is possible to break a crystal glass by singing a certain note.

☐ ☐ It is possible to travel faster than the speed of sound.

2 Draw A person standing on the edge of a canyon can make an echo by calling into the canyon. Draw how you think the sound waves travel to make the echo. Use arrows to represent the direction of the sound waves.

Active Reading

3 Synthesize You can often determine the meaning of a term when you have heard some of the words in a different context. Draw a line from the terms on the left to their description on the right.

• constructive interference   • causes sound waves to get smaller

• destructive interference   • causes sound waves to get larger

Vocabulary Terms

• echo   • resonance
• interference

4 Apply As you learn the definition of each vocabulary term in this lesson, create your own definition or sketch to help you remember the meaning of the term.

Some Like It Hot

What affects the speed of sound?

Have you ever seen a flash of lightning, and then heard the sound of thunder a few seconds later? That happens because sound travels more slowly than light. Two main factors affect the speed of sound: the type of medium that the sound travels through, and the temperature of the medium. If we know these factors, we can predict the speed of sound.

Medium

The speed of sound depends on the type of matter, or medium, through which the sound wave travels. When you swim or bathe, you can hear sounds in more than one medium—air and water. The state of matter affects the speed of sound as well. In general, sound travels fastest through solids, slower through liquids, and slowest through gases. Sound travels fastest through solids because solids are denser than liquids or gases. That means that the particles are packed closer together in solids. A sound wave makes the particles of matter move as it travels along, so the wave is fastest when particles are close together.

Active Reading

5 Explain How does the state of matter affect the speed of sound?

_____

_____

_____

Visualize It!

6 Identify Through what medium shown below does sound travel fastest? _____

Slowest? _____

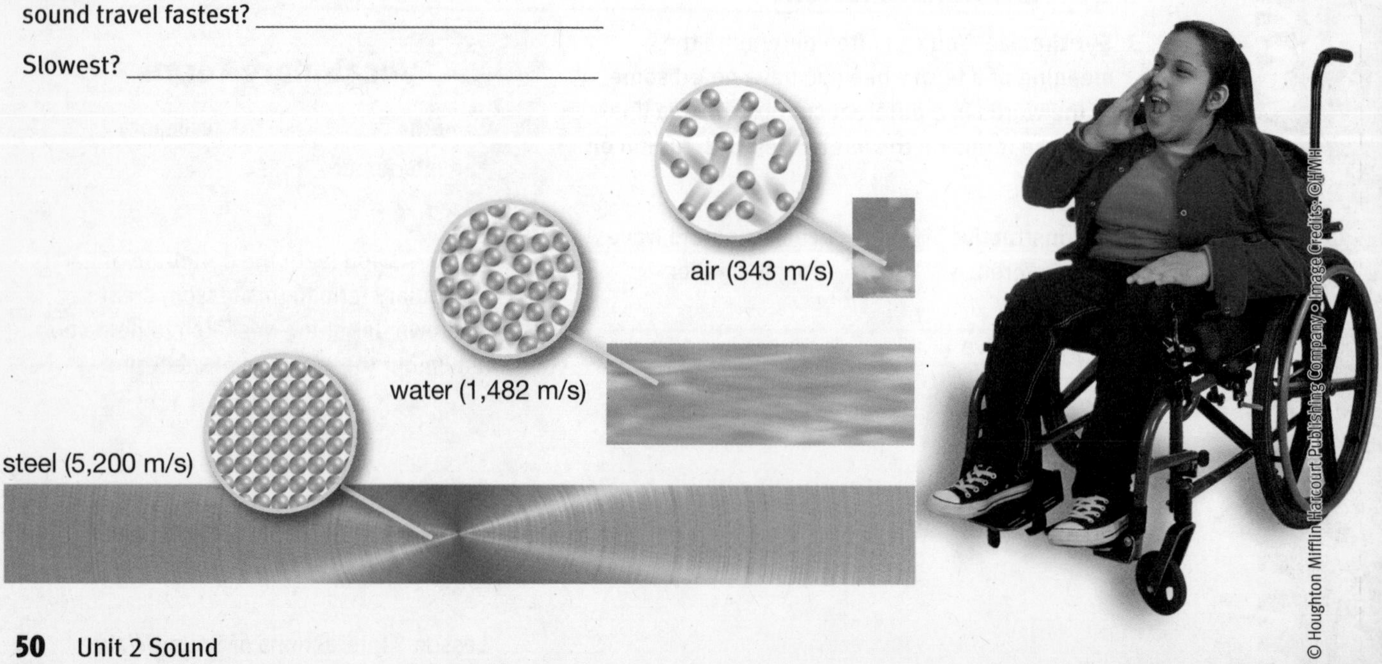

air (343 m/s)

water (1,482 m/s)

steel (5,200 m/s)

Temperature

The speed of sound also depends on the temperature of a medium. Sound in a medium travels faster at higher temperatures than at lower ones. Consider air, which is a mixture of gases. Particles in a gas are not held together as tightly as particles in a solid are. Instead, the gas particles bounce all around. The higher the temperature, the faster the gas particles move about. Particles of a material move more quickly and transfer energy faster at higher temperatures than at lower temperatures. Therefore, sound travels faster through hot air than through cold air.

Do the Math

Sample Problem

Sound travels at 343 m/s through air at a temperature of 20 °C. How far will sound travel through 20 °C air in 5 s?

$$343 \text{ m}/1 \text{ s} = X \text{ m}/5 \text{ s}$$
$$343 \text{ m} \times 5 = X \text{ m}$$
$$X \text{ m} = 1{,}715 \text{ m}$$

You Try It

7 **Calculate** The speed of sound in steel at 20 °C is 5,200 m/s. How far can sound travel in 5 s through steel at 20 °C?

8 **Apply** Who will hear the sound of an approaching boat first: this diver or his friends above the water? Why?

_____

_____

_____

Speed of Sound in Different Media and Temperatures	
Medium	**Speed (m/s)**
Air (0 °C)	331
Air (20 °C)	343
Air (100 °C)	366
Water (20 °C)	1,482
Steel (20 °C)	5,200

Hello? Hello? Hello?

How do sound and matter interact?

Sound waves do not travel easily through all matter. When a sound wave runs into a barrier, some of the sound waves may bounce away from the front surface of the barrier, and some of the sound waves may be absorbed or transmitted through the barrier.

Matter Can Reflect Sound Waves

Sound waves, like all waves, can reflect off matter. Reflection is the bouncing back of a wave when the wave hits a barrier. The strength of a reflected sound wave depends on the reflecting surface. Sound waves reflect best off smooth, hard surfaces. A sound in a bare room can be loud because the sound waves are reflected off the walls, the floor, and the ceiling. If furniture, drapes, and carpet are added to the room, the same sound is much softer.

Matter Can Absorb Sound Waves

Some types of matter absorb sound waves much better than others. A rough wall will absorb sound better than a smooth wall will. And soft materials absorb sound better than hard materials do. If your school has a music room, it probably has sound-absorbing features, such as carpet and soft, rough acoustic tiles on walls and ceilings. These features help keep the music from being heard throughout the school.

Visualize It!

10 Identify Which features in this room reflect sound waves? Explain your reasoning.

_____

_____

_____

_____

_____

The surfaces in room A interact differently with sound waves than do the surfaces in room B.

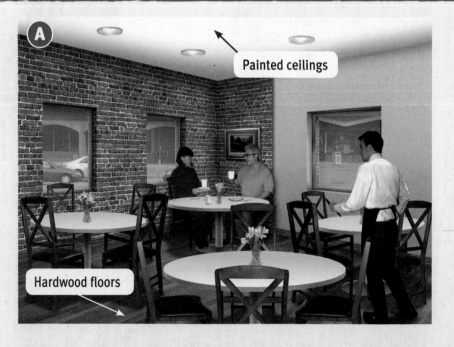

A

Painted ceilings

Hardwood floors

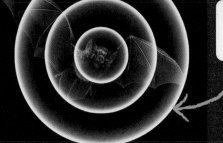

1 The sound waves that bats emit while flying are at a higher frequency than humans can hear.

Bats use echoes to navigate.

2 The sound waves meet an object and reflect back to the bat. The time it takes these echoes to reach the bat tells it how far the object is.

3 The bat can determine the direction an insect is flying in because the frequency of the echo changes as the insect moves.

What is an echo?

Matter that absorbs sound waves will reduce echoes. An **echo** is a reflected sound wave. The strength of a reflecting sound wave depends on the reflecting surface. Echoes can be reduced by the presence of soft materials and rough or irregular surfaces. Rough surfaces reduce echoes by scattering sound waves.

Some animals—such as dolphins, bats, and beluga whales—use echoes to hunt food and to find objects in their paths. The use of reflected sound waves to find objects is called *echolocation*. The illustrations on this page show how echolocation works. Animals that use echolocation can tell how far away something is based on how long it takes sound waves to echo back to the animal.

One example of echolocation technology used by people is sonar (**s**ound **n**avigation **a**nd **r**anging). *Sonar* is a type of electronic echolocation that uses echoes to locate objects underwater.

Active Reading **11 Describe** How do some animals use echoes?

_____

_____

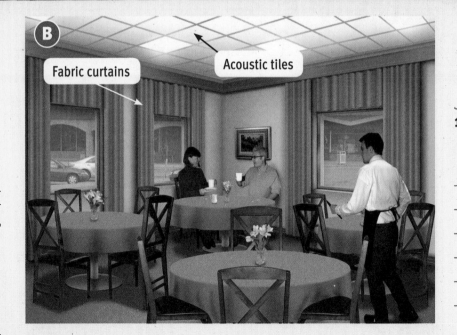

B

Fabric curtains

Acoustic tiles

12 Describe Explain how the features in this room help reduce echoes.

_____

_____

_____

_____

_____

_____

Boom!

How do sound waves interact with each other?

Sound waves interact through interference. **Interference** happens when two or more waves overlap and combine to form one wave. In music, *beats* happen when two sound waves of nearly equal frequencies interfere. Since the wave frequencies are not quite equal, they form a repeating pattern of constructive and destructive interference that sounds alternately loud and soft.

Active Reading 13 **Identify** As you read, underline the main characteristics of constructive interference and destructive interference.

Through Constructive Interference

When *constructive interference* occurs, waves overlap and combine to form a wave with a larger amplitude, or height. The greater amplitude causes the waves to produce a sound that is louder than before. Constructive interference can cause very loud sounds, such as sonic booms.

Through Destructive Interference

In *destructive interference,* waves combine to form a wave with a smaller amplitude. The sound will be softer because the amplitude is decreased. Some noise-canceling headphones use destructive interference. Electronics in the headphones create new sound waves that interfere with outside sounds, so the headphone wearer does not hear them.

When two speakers produce sound at the same frequency, the sound waves combine by both constructive and destructive interference.

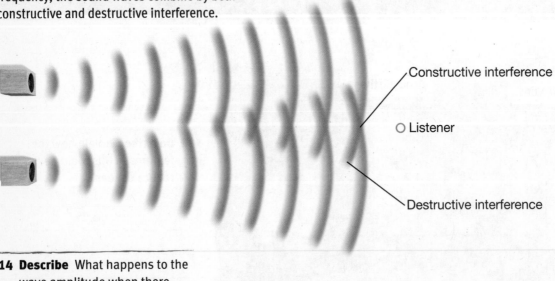

Constructive interference

O Listener

Destructive interference

14 Describe What happens to the wave amplitude when there is constructive interference? What happens when destructive interference occurs?

_____

_____

_____

© Houghton Mifflin Harcourt Publishing Company • Image Credits: (bg) ©Navy News/PhotoReuters/Corbis

How does interference cause sonic booms?

Jet airplanes moving faster than the speed of sound can produce a very loud sound called a *sonic boom*. The sonic boom from a low-flying airplane can rattle and even break windows! When a jet reaches very high speeds, it actually catches up to its own sound waves. The waves pile up as a result of constructive interference. They form a high-pressure area, called the *sound barrier,* in front of the plane. If the jet is going fast enough, it breaks through the barrier. The jet moves at *supersonic* speeds—speeds faster than the speed of sound—and gets ahead of both the pressure barrier and the sound waves. The sound waves behind the jet form a single shock wave as a result of constructive interference. When the shock wave reaches people's ears, they hear it as a loud boom!

Traveling at very high speeds, a jet can break through a barrier of its own sound waves.

Visualize It!

15 Identify Draw an arrow on the top image to indicate where the sound barrier is.

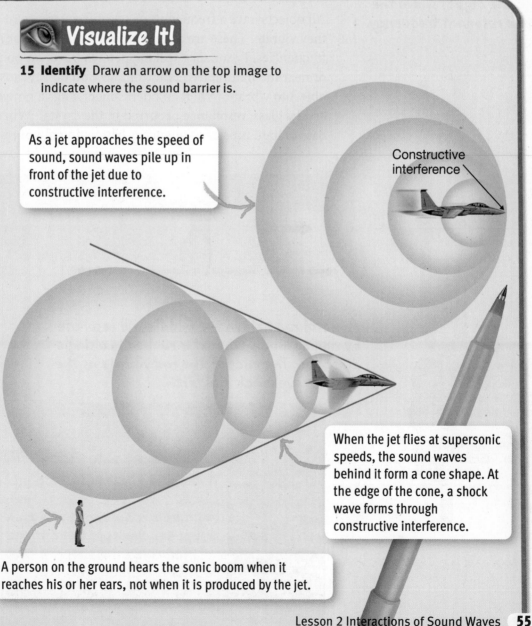

As a jet approaches the speed of sound, sound waves pile up in front of the jet due to constructive interference.

Constructive interference

When the jet flies at supersonic speeds, the sound waves behind it form a cone shape. At the edge of the cone, a shock wave forms through constructive interference.

A person on the ground hears the sonic boom when it reaches his or her ears, not when it is produced by the jet.

Good Vibrations

Active Reading

16 **Identify** As you read, underline the main characteristics of resonance.

What is resonance?

Have you ever held a seashell to your ear and listened to the "ocean"? What you actually are hearing is resonance. **Resonance** happens when a sound wave matches the natural frequency of an object and causes the object to vibrate. The air in the seashell vibrates at certain frequencies because of the shape of the shell. If a sound wave in the room forces air in the seashell to vibrate at its natural frequency, resonance occurs. This resonance results in a big vibration that sounds like the ocean when you hear it.

Where can resonance occur?

All objects have a frequency, or set of frequencies, at which they vibrate. These are called *natural frequencies,* or *resonant* frequencies. Resonance will happen wherever an object vibrating at or near the natural frequency of a second object causes the second object to vibrate. When an opera singer sings a note that breaks a crystal glass, resonance occurred in the crystal. When you feel the bass of loud music, resonance is happening in your body.

A vibrating tuning fork can cause another object to start vibrating if the fork and the object share the same resonant frequency.

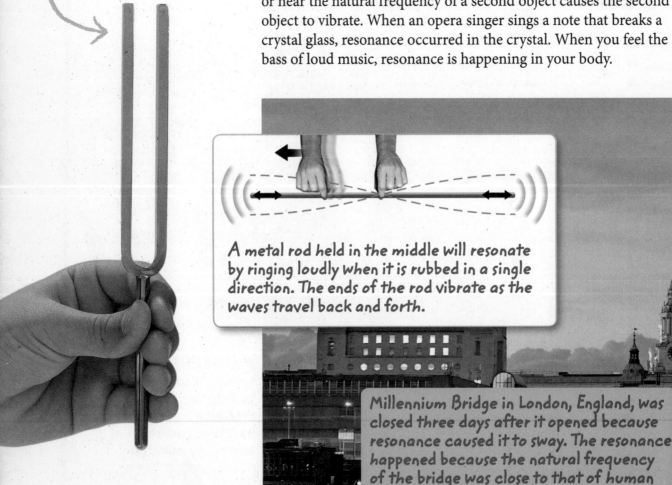

A metal rod held in the middle will resonate by ringing loudly when it is rubbed in a single direction. The ends of the rod vibrate as the waves travel back and forth.

Millennium Bridge in London, England, was closed three days after it opened because resonance caused it to sway. The resonance happened because the natural frequency of the bridge was close to that of human footsteps walking across it.

In Musical Instruments

Active Reading **17 Identify** As you read, underline how resonance occurs in wind instruments.

Resonance is important for making music. In wind instruments, blowing air into the mouthpiece causes vibrations. The vibrations make a sound that gets louder when it forms a standing wave inside the instrument. A *standing wave* is a pattern of vibration that looks like a wave that is standing still. Resonance occurs when standing waves are formed. Waves and reflected waves of the same frequency go back and forth in standing waves inside the instrument.

String instruments also resonate when played. An acoustic guitar has a hollow body. When the strings make a standing wave, the sound waves enter the body of the guitar. Standing waves also form inside the body, and the sound becomes louder.

In Bridges

Resonance can even occur in buildings, towers, and bridges. Because resonance could cause a structure to collapse, engineers plan their designs carefully. For example, some bridges are built in sections with overlapping plates. When the plates move together, they create friction. This friction can change the frequency from one plate to another and keep the resonant wave from becoming destructive. Even simple human activity can create resonance on bridges. For example, rhythmic marching can create resonance and cause a bridge to sway or even collapse. That's why troops always stop marching before crossing a bridge.

This musician creates music by making standing waves on the strings of her cello.

Think Outside the Book (Inquiry)

18 Apply To better understand how marching can resonate with bridges, form a line with your classmates and march in time around your classroom. As you march, try to be aware of the vibrations and resonance of the classroom floor. Then repeat, but "break step"—march out of time. Do the floor and other objects respond the way they did in the first trial?

Visual Summary

To complete this summary, fill in the word to finish each sentence. Then, use the key below to check your answers. You can use this page to review the main concepts of the lesson.

Interactions of Sound Waves

The speed of sound depends on the medium it travels through and on the temperature of the medium.

Sound waves interact with each other through interference.

19 Sound waves travel _____ in solids than in liquids.

20 _____ interference occurs when sound waves meet and form a wave that makes a quieter sound.

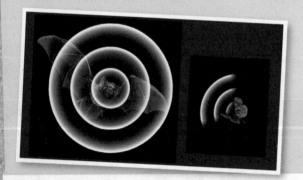

Some surfaces reflect sound waves, while other surfaces absorb sound waves.

Resonance occurs when the frequency of a sound wave matches the natural frequency of an object and makes the object vibrate.

21 Sound waves reflect better off _____ surfaces.

22 Resonance happens when two objects vibrate at _____ frequency.

23 Summarize What are the results of the two ways that sound waves can interact with each other?

Lesson Review

Vocabulary

Fill in the blank with the term that best completes the following sentence.

1 _____ is the combination of two or more waves, which results in a single wave.

2 _____ happens when a sound wave causes an object to vibrate.

3 A(n) _____ is a reflected sound wave.

Key Concepts

4 Identify How does the state of matter affect the speed of a sound wave traveling through it?

_____

_____

_____

_____

5 Describe How could you reduce the echoes in a music studio?

_____

_____

_____

_____

6 Explain Describe how a jet can create a sonic boom.

_____

_____

_____

_____

7 Summarize In your own words, explain how resonance occurs when you play a horn.

_____

_____

_____

_____

_____

Critical Thinking

Use this table to answer the following questions.

Speed of Sound in Some Materials	
Material	**Speed of sound (m/s)**
air	330
water	1,480
brain	1,540
blood	1,570

8 Analyze Ultrasound uses high-frequency sound waves to get images of the insides of our bodies. Sound waves would travel the fastest through which of the materials listed in the chart?

_____

_____

9 Infer What two types of matter are closest in density? How do you know?

_____

_____

_____

_____

10 Relate Ultrasound waves do not transmit easily through bone. What do you think happens to ultrasound waves when they reach a bone in the body? Give reasons for your answer.

_____

_____

_____

_____

_____

_____

_____

My Notes

James West

RESEARCH SCIENTIST

James West's parents wanted him to be a medical doctor, but he wanted to study physics. His father was sure he'd never find a job that way. But Dr. West wanted to study what he loved. He did study physics, and he did find a job. He worked for Bell Laboratories and developed a microphone called the electret microphone. Today, Dr. West's microphone is in almost all telephones, cell phones, and other equipment that records sound.

Dr. West's interest in the microphone started with a question about hearing. A group of scientists wanted to know how close together two sounds could be before the ear would not be able to tell them apart. At the time, there was no earphone sensitive enough for their tests. Dr. West and fellow scientist Dr. Gerhard Sessler found that they could make a more sensitive microphone by using materials called *electrets*. Electrets are the electrical counterparts of permanent magnets. Some metals can become magnetic. Electrets can store electric charge. This eliminates the need for a battery. The new microphones were cheaper, more reliable, smaller, and lighter than any microphone before them.

Dr. West enjoys the thrill of discovery. He should know. To date, he holds more than 200 U.S. and foreign patents. In 1999 he was inducted into the National Inventors Hall of Fame. Dr. West retired from Bell Laboratories in 2001 and is now on the faculty at Johns Hopkins University. He has won many awards for his work, including both the Silver and Gold Medals from the Acoustical Society of America, the National Medal of Technology, and the Benjamin Franklin Medal in Electrical Engineering.

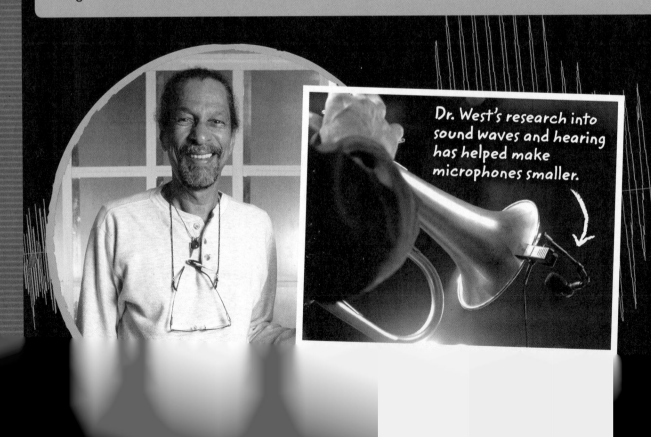

Dr. West's research into sound waves and hearing has helped make microphones smaller.

JOB BOARD

Dispensing Optician

What You'll Do: Help select and then fit eyeglasses and contact lenses.

Where You Might Work: Medical offices, or optical, department, or club stores

Education: Most training is on the job or through apprenticeships that last two years or longer. Some employers prefer graduates of postsecondary training programs in opticianry.

Other Job Requirements: A good eye for fashion, face shape, and color is a plus, as opticians help people find glasses they like.

Lighting Designer

What You'll Do: Work in theater, television, or film to make what happens on stage or on set visible to audiences. Lighting designers also use lighting and shadow to create the right tone or mood.

Where You Might Work: Theaters, television and film studios and sets, concerts and other special events

Education: A diploma or certificate in lighting design or technical stage management from a college or performing arts institute

Other Job Requirements: Experience lighting stage productions, the ability to work in a team

ELY Stone

A New Light on Microscopy

Doctors and medical researchers use fluorescent microscopes to see colored or fluorescent dyes in medical research. These microscopes use expensive and dangerous mercury light bulbs to illuminate the dyes. But Ely Stone, a retired computer programmer and inventor in Florida, found a less expensive source of light.

When the mercury bulb on his microscope died, Ely replaced it with many differently colored light-emitting diodes (LEDs). Each inexpensive LED emits light of a different wavelength. The LEDs cost only a couple of dollars each and are much safer than mercury bulbs. Yet they still provide the light needed to view the fluorescent dyes. Now, researchers can use the LED microscopes to really light up their dyes!

Sound Technology

ESSENTIAL QUESTION

How does sound technology work?

By the end of this lesson, you should be able to describe how sound technology is used to extend human senses.

Many radio programs are recorded so that you can listen to them whenever you want.

Lesson Labs

Quick Labs
- Sound Recording and Playback
- Making an AM Radio Transmitter

Engage Your Brain

1 Predict Check T or F to show whether you think each statement is true or false.

T	F	
☐	☐	Some animals use sound to find food.
☐	☐	Reflected sound waves can be used to make images.
☐	☐	Sound waves are sent from one telephone to another telephone.
☐	☐	Computers can save and store sound waves.

2 Describe List three devices that produce sound waves that you use in your everyday life. Describe how your life would be different without these devices.

Active Reading

3 Synthesize You can often define an unknown word if you know the meaning of its word parts. Use the word part and sentence below to make an educated guess about the meaning of the word *ultrasound*.

Word Part	Meaning
ultra-	beyond

Example sentence
Humans cannot hear <u>ultrasound</u> waves.

ultrasound:

Vocabulary Terms

- **echolocation**
- **sonar**
- **ultrasound**

4 Apply As you learn the definition of each vocabulary term in this lesson, create your own definition or sketch to help you remember the meaning of the term.

How are echoes used?

You would have difficulty using your sense of hearing to find objects around you. But some animals find food and other objects using *echolocation*. **Echolocation** is the use of echoes, or reflected sound waves to find objects. Animals that use echolocation produce **ultrasound**, which are sound waves that have frequencies greater than 20,000 Hz. The frequencies of these ultrasonic sound waves are too high for humans to hear. But, animals that use echolocation can tell how far away an object is by the time it takes for their ultrasonic waves to bounce off an object and return to them, or *echo*. For example, the dolphin shown below can tell how far away the fish is by sensing the echoes that bounce off of the fish. It takes more time for ultrasonic sound waves to reach and return from objects that are farther away.

 **Active Reading** **5 Explain** What are ultrasonic waves?

_____

_____

Visualize It!

6 Illustrate Draw the sound waves that are reflected from the fish.

7 Analyze Will the echo from the fish or from the boat reach the dolphin first?

_____

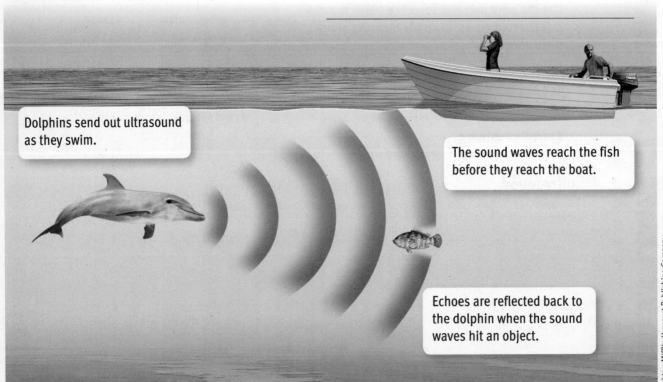

Dolphins send out ultrasound as they swim.

The sound waves reach the fish before they reach the boat.

Echoes are reflected back to the dolphin when the sound waves hit an object.

To Locate Objects

You may not be able to send out or hear ultrasonic waves, but people can use echolocation through various technologies. **Sonar** is a system that uses sound waves to determine the location of objects or to communicate. Visually impaired people can use sonar technology to navigate. Sonar is also used to find shipwrecks, to avoid icebergs, to find fish, and to map the ocean floor as shown in this diagram. An instrument on the boat sends out ultrasonic waves. Then it detects any echoes, or reflected sound waves. The short wavelengths of ultrasonic waves provide more information about objects than the longer wavelengths of sound do.

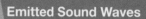

Emitted Sound Waves

Reflected sound waves are used to map the ocean floor. The red areas are closer to the ship. The blue areas are farther away.

A *more time / less time*

Reflected Sound Waves

B *more time / less time*

 Visualize It!

8 Label Circle the correct phrase in each box on the map to show where the reflected sound waves will take more time to return to the ship and where they will take less time to return to the ship.

To Make Ultrasound Images

Echoes are used in medicine, too. Ultrasound procedures use ultrasonic sound waves to produce images of the inside of a person's body. Ultrasound that has a frequency of 1 million to 10 million hertz can pass safely into a patient's body. These sound waves reflect when they meet the patient's internal organs. The echoes are detected and used to make images of organs, such as the heart and bladder. Ultrasonic waves do not damage human cells like x-rays can. Ultrasound procedures do not harm fetuses. So ultrasound is often used to check how a fetus is growing inside the mother's body. Health professionals can use ultrasound images to determine the age and sex of a fetus and to diagnose certain disorders.

This ultrasound image shows a 20-week-old fetus.

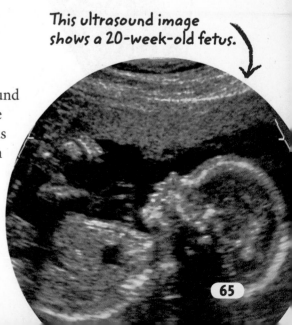

How do telephones transmit sound?

📖 **Active Reading**

9 Identify As you read, underline the types of signals sound waves are changed into by telephones.

Sound waves lose energy over time. The sound waves of your voice will not reach a friend who is far away. But, you can use a telephone to talk to your friend. Phones change sound waves into other types of signals that can be sent over long distances. Phones also change the signals they receive back into sound waves that you can hear.

All telephones change sound waves into electrical signals. However, electrical signals cannot travel through air. So, in the case of cordless phones, the handset and the base change electrical signals into radio waves that they transmit to each other. These radio waves travel at the speed of light. The base then changes the radio waves back to electrical signals that are sent through wires. A computer sends these signals to the phone of the other caller, where they are changed back into sound waves.

The **microphone** in the mouthpiece changes the sound waves from your voice into electrical signals. These electrical signals are then changed into radio waves that are sent to the phone base.

The **earpiece** turns electrical signals into sound waves. The sound you hear is very similar to the sound that was spoken into the phone of the other caller.

The **phone base** receives radio signals from the handset. It changes them into electrical signals. It also receives incoming electrical signals from the wall outlet, which it changes into radio waves that are sent to the handset.

Radio waves

Phone wires send electrical signals outside of the house to a switching station that connects callers. Incoming signals also travel along the wires to the base.

Think Outside the Book (Inquiry)

10 Apply Create a short cartoon with captions that shows the changes the sound waves go through during a telephone call.

Hello, Operator

For most of human history, people had no way of sending their voices farther than they could shout. The invention of the telephone in 1876 made long-distance communication possible. How has telephone technology changed since then?

Manual Switching

People used to have to call telephone operators whenever they wanted to make a call. The operator plugged wires into a switchboard to connect one phone to another. The switchboard allowed many phone calls to be connected at one time.

Dialing Around

The invention of the rotary dial phone made it possible for people to call a number directly. Human operators were replaced by automated switching centers.

Cell Phones

Modern cell phones use radio waves to send signals. The signals are sent to cell phone towers, which transfer the signals to underground phone cables. Cell phones can also send images and text.

Extend

Inquiry

11 Infer What was a main advantage of a dial phone over an operator-controlled switchboard?

12 Research Make a timeline that shows the following major inventions related to telephones: the telephone, the telephone switching center, the rotary phone, the push-button phone, and the mobile phone. Include pictures and an interesting detail about each invention in your timeline.

13 Compose Write a short paragraph describing how you use telephones in your everyday life. Include one way you would improve your phone.

Groovy

How is sound recorded and played back?

Once sound waves lose their energy, they are gone forever. People make recordings to preserve sound information, such as interviews and music. Thomas Edison invented the phonograph, which could record and play back sound. Later, information in sound was recorded in the grooves of records. Today, most sound recordings are stored on compact discs or in computer files.

Active Reading

14 Identify As you read, underline why people record sound.

Music can be stored in the grooves of records.

On Compact Discs

A compact disc, or CD, is made of hard plastic. The information in sound waves is stored by pressing microscopic pits into the plastic. The pits and lands, which are the spaces between the pits, form a spiral pattern on the CD. This pattern stores digital signals as 1s and 0s that are used to recreate sound waves.

A CD player uses light to read the information stored on the CD. The plastic layer of a CD is coated with a thin layer of shiny aluminum. The light from a laser reflects off the shiny surface as the CD rotates. The pattern on the CD surface produces a pattern of light and dark reflected light. The detector changes this pattern into an electrical signal. The CD player then changes the electrical signal back into sound waves.

Visualize It!

This image shows the pattern on the surface of a CD. Different patterns produce different sounds. CD players use reflected light to read the pattern on CDs.

Compact disc

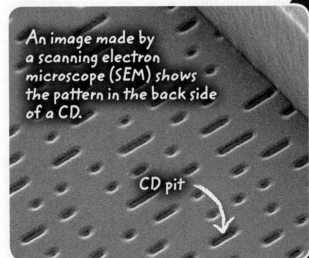

An image made by a scanning electron microscope (SEM) shows the pattern in the back side of a CD.

CD pit

15 Analyze Suppose the pattern near the arrow represents part of a word of an audio book. How do you think the pattern will appear on the CD the next time that word is repeated? Explain.

_____

_____

_____

_____

_____

In Computers

Sound can also be stored as digital files in a computer. Digital sound files, such as MP3 files, can store a large amount of sound information. To record sound as a computer file, the original sound is first changed into an electrical signal. Then it is stored as a digital file on the computer hard drive. The digital file is a series of 1s and 0s, similar to the pattern stored on a CD.

Software reads the digital files and produces an electrical signal that is sent to the speakers. The speakers change the signal back into sound waves. Personal MP3 players store and play back sound files in a similar way as larger computers do. But they make it very easy to carry a lot of recordings with you. You would need several CDs to store the hundreds of songs that can be stored in a tiny MP3 player.

Sound is stored in digital files in computers.

16 Summarize Complete the following process chart to show how sound waves can be digitally recorded and played back.

Original sound waves are played.			Sound waves come out of speaker.

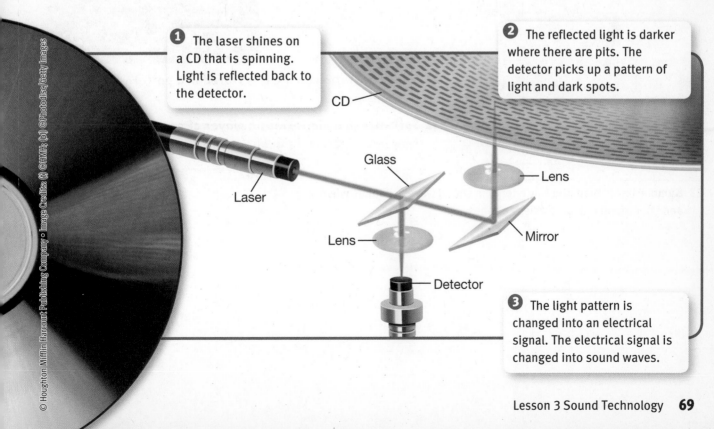

❶ The laser shines on a CD that is spinning. Light is reflected back to the detector.

❷ The reflected light is darker where there are pits. The detector picks up a pattern of light and dark spots.

CD

Laser

Glass

Lens

Lens

Mirror

Detector

❸ The light pattern is changed into an electrical signal. The electrical signal is changed into sound waves.

Visual Summary

To complete this summary, circle the correct word or phrase. Then, use the key below to check your answers. You can use this page to review the main concepts of the lesson.

Echolocation is the use of ultrasound to locate objects.

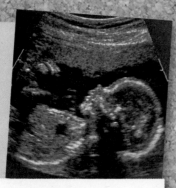

17 A fetus can be viewed using an infrasound / ultrasound procedure.

18 Sonar / Laser light is used to locate objects underwater.

Telephones change sound waves into electrical signals and electrical signals back into sound waves.

19 A cordless phone sends sound / radio waves between the handset and the base.

20 A telephone's earpiece / microphone changes sound waves into electrical signals.

Sound Technology

Sound information is stored digitally on compact discs and in computer files.

21 The information on a CD is stored in a pattern of pits and lands / light waves.

22 Software in a digital music player changes music files into electrical signals / radio waves.

Answers: 17 ultrasound; 18 Sonar; 19 radio; 20 microphone; 21 pits and lands; 22 electrical signals

23 **Summarize** Explain the way energy in sound waves changes when you and your friend talk on cordless phones.

Lesson Review

Vocabulary

In your own words, define the following terms.

1 echolocation

_____

_____

2 ultrasound

_____

_____

3 sonar

_____

_____

Key Concepts

4 Identify Which device can store sound information?

   A CD player

   B telephone wires

   C microphone

   D computer

5 Describe How does a telephone handset change the incoming signals from a caller into sound that you can hear?

_____

_____

_____

6 Infer Why do people use echolocation technology to locate objects?

_____

_____

_____

7 Explain Why are sound recordings needed to preserve sound information?

_____

_____

_____

Critical Thinking

8 Explain Describe what happens inside a CD player when you listen to an audio CD.

_____

_____

_____

_____

9 Apply Explain how a doctor can use ultrasound to look at a patient's kidneys.

_____

_____

_____

_____

Use this drawing to answer the following questions.

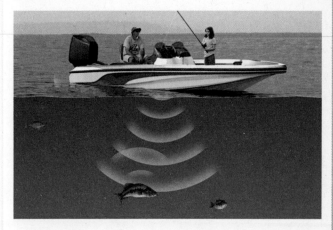

10 Describe How is sound technology being used by the people in the boat?

_____

_____

11 Analyze Why are the sound waves in the drawing shown to be reflecting from the larger fish but not from the smaller fish under the boat?

_____

_____

_____

My Notes

Unit 2 Big Idea ◄ Sound waves transfer energy through vibrations.

Lesson 1
ESSENTIAL QUESTION
What is sound?

Describe what sound is, identify its properties, and explain how humans hear it.

Lesson 2
ESSENTIAL QUESTION
How do sound waves travel and interact?

Describe how sound waves interact, and how they can cause echoes and sonic booms.

Lesson 3
ESSENTIAL QUESTION
How does sound technology work?

Describe how sound technology is used to extend human senses.

Connect **ESSENTIAL QUESTIONS**
Lessons 1 and 2

1 Synthesize If you bounce a basketball in an empty gym, you will hear it echo. Describe the path that the sound wave travels from the basketball to your eardrum.

_____

_____

_____

_____

Think Outside the Book

2 Synthesize Choose one of these activities to help synthesize what you have learned in this unit.

☐ Using what you learned in lessons 2 and 3, create a brochure to sell a sound absorbing material, explaining why recording studios need this material for the walls and ceiling. Use illustrations with captions and labels.

☐ Using what you learned in lessons 1 and 3, make a poster to explain why communicating in space is a challenge, and show how space scientists have met this challenge.

74 Unit 2 Sound

© Houghton Mifflin Harcourt Publishing Company • Image Credits: (tl) ©Tim Pannell/Corbis; (tr) ©Tim Flach/Stone+/Getty Images; (b) ©Inti St Clair/Blend Images/Getty Images

Unit 2 Review

Name _____

Vocabulary

Check the box to show whether each statement is true or false.

T	F	
☐	☐	**1** A Sound wave is a <u>longitudinal wave</u> that is caused by vibrations in a medium.
☐	☐	**2** <u>Decibels</u> are units that measure the pitch of a sound.
☐	☐	**3** An <u>echo</u> is a sound wave that is absorbed by a soft material.
☐	☐	**4** <u>Interference</u> occurs when two or more waves overlap and combine to form one wave.
☐	☐	**5** <u>Ultrasound</u> technology is used to create medical images and it is based on sound waves with frequencies so high that human ears cannot hear them.

Key Concepts

Read each question below, and circle the best answer.

6 Which statement best describes how humans hear sound?

A Sound waves enter the ear canal and increase in amplitude, which causes you to hear the sound.

B Sound waves cause parts of the ear to vibrate until the waves are converted to electrical signals, which are sent to the brain.

C Sound waves travel into people's ears, and the eardrum sends the sound waves to the brain.

D Sound waves become sounds when they strike the eardrum inside the ear.

7 When Consuelo struck a tuning fork and held it close to a string on a guitar, the string began to vibrate on its own and make a sound. Which statement best explains why the string vibrated without anyone touching it?

A The string vibrated because of destructive inference between its sound waves and those of the tuning fork.

B The tuning fork produced ultrasonic frequencies beyond human hearing.

C The tuning fork and the guitar string both created mechanical waves.

D The string vibrated because of resonance, which happened because the tuning fork and guitar string have the same natural frequency.

8 The diagram below shows a sound wave traveling through a medium.

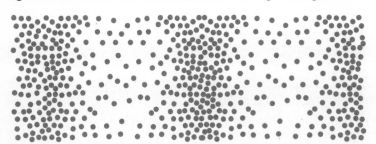

Which statement best describes how the sound wave is moving through a medium?

A The sound wave is creating tensions and accumulations in the medium.

B The sound wave is creating an echo inside the medium.

C The sound wave is creating compressions and rarefactions in the medium.

D The sound wave is creating a mechanical wave in the medium.

9 Which material best absorbs sound waves in a room?

A heavy curtains   **C** brick walls

B hardwood floors   **D** cement floors

10 Yorgos drew a diagram of a wave and labeled its parts, as shown below.

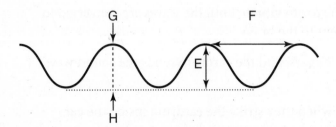

Wavelength is typically measured between the crests to two successive waves. Which labels represent a crest and a wavelength?

A G points to a crest; F is a wavelength

B G points to a crest; E is a wavelength

C H points to a crest; E is a wavelength

D H points to a crest; F is a wavelength

11 Which of the following is not a way in which echolocation is used?

A flying bats avoiding trees and houses at night

B sending messages over telephone lines

C dolphins finding fish in deep water

D mapping the ocean floor

12 Josh observed a bolt of lightning during a thunderstorm. It took more than 15 seconds for Josh to hear the sound of thunder. Why did Josh see the lighting strike before he heard the thunder?

A Thunder always takes 15 seconds to travel through the air after lighting strikes.

B Light waves from the lightning and sound waves from the thunder moved through different media.

C Light waves are electromagnetic waves that travel much faster than mechanical waves, such as the sound waves he heard as thunder.

D The conditions in the air at the time allowed light waves to move faster than the sound waves he heard as thunder.

13 The diagram below shows the distribution of particles in two different kinds of media.

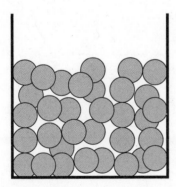 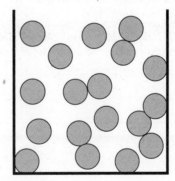

Which statement best compares how sound waves travel through the media shown above?

A Sound waves travel at the same speed through both of the media shown.

B Sound waves move faster through the closely packed medium on the left than the loosely packed medium on the right.

C Sound waves move faster through the loosely packed medium on the right than the closely packed medium on the left.

D Sound waves cannot travel through either medium that is shown above.

Critical Thinking

Answer the following questions in the space provided.

14 Describe where the cochlea is located, what parts it contains, and explain the role these parts play in human hearing.

_____

_____

_____

15 Suppose you are at a train station. What changes would you hear in the sound of the whistle as a train comes toward you and then moves away? What causes the changes, and what is this effect called?

_____

_____

_____

_____

Connect **ESSENTIAL QUESTIONS**
Lessons 1 and 2

16 A fighter jet breaks the sound barrier. What is the sound barrier, and how can a jet break through it? Where does the sound around the jet come from? What causes the sonic boom, and how can you hear it?

_____

_____

_____

_____

_____

Light

Big Idea

Visible light is the small part of the electromagnetic spectrum that is essential for human vision.

What do you think?

Waves can travel great distances. This large radio telescope gathers radio waves from space. Other telescopes use mirrors to gather light waves. What have people learned about space from light waves?

Looking Into Space

The first telescopes were refracting telescopes, which used a pair of lenses to gather light. Today, astronomers also use reflecting telescopes, which gather light with large mirrors, to observe distant objects.

Galileo observing space

1609
Galileo Galilei used a refracting telescope to observe phases of Venus, the moons of Jupiter, the surface of the moon, sunspots, and a supernova.

List other tools that use lenses and think of a use for each one.

_____

_____

_____

_____

_____

Telescope similar to Isaac Newton's

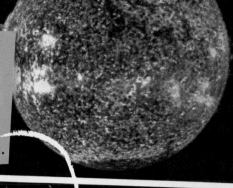

Skylab image of the sun

1973

Telescopes that operate from space, like the sun-observing telescope that was aboard Skylab, can see all kinds of things we can't see from Earth.

1668

Isaac Newton built a reflecting telescope that used a curved mirror to gather light. Newton's mirror did not split light into colors as did the lenses in early refracting telescopes.

1990

The orbiting Hubble Space Telescope can capture detailed images of objects very far from Earth. The Hubble Space Telescope has taken images of the most distant galaxies astronomers have ever seen.

Hubble Space Telescope

Take It Home   Eyes to the Sky

Use a pair of binoculars or a telescope to look at the night sky. Compare what you can see with magnification to what you can see when looking at the same part of the sky without magnification. Draw or write your observations in the chart.

Unmagnified Night Sky	Magnified Night Sky

The Electromagnetic Spectrum

ESSENTIAL QUESTION

What is the relationship between various EM waves?

By the end of this lesson, you should be able to distinguish between the parts of the electromagnetic spectrum.

This iron glows with EM radiation that we normally can't see. The brighter areas represent hotter parts of the iron.

Engage Your Brain

1 Select Circle the word or phrase that best completes each of the following sentences:

Radio stations transmit (*radio waves/gamma rays*).

The dentist uses (*infrared light/x-rays*) to examine your teeth.

Intense (*visible light/ultraviolet light*) from the sun can damage your skin.

2 Predict Imagine that humans had not realized there are other parts of the electromagnetic spectrum besides visible light. How would your day today be different without technology based on other parts of the EM spectrum?

_____

_____

_____

_____

_____

Active Reading

3 Synthesize You can often define an unknown word if you know the meaning of its word parts. Use this table of word parts to make an educated guess about the meanings given.

Word part	Meaning
ultra-	beyond
infra-	below
electro-	related to electricty
-magnetic	related to magnetism

What word means "beyond violet"?

_____

What word means "below red"?

_____

What word means "related to electricity and magnetism"?

_____

Vocabulary Terms
- Radiation
- Electromagnetic spectrum
- Infrared
- Ultraviolet

4 Apply As you learn the definition of each vocabulary term in this lesson, think of an example of a real-world use. Practice writing the term and its definition, and then writing or drawing a sketch of the example next to the definition.

Electromagnetic Light Show

What is the nature of light?

Light is a type of energy that travels as waves, but light waves are not disturbances in a medium. Light waves are disturbances in electric and magnetic fields. If you have felt the static cling of fabric and the pull of a magnet, then you have experienced electric and magnetic fields. Because these fields can exist in empty space, light does not need a medium in which to travel.

When an electrically charged particle vibrates, it disturbs the electric and magnetic fields around it. These disturbances, called electromagnetic (EM) waves, carry energy away from the charged particle. The disturbances are perpendicular to each other and to the direction the wave travels. **Radiation** (ray•dee•AY•shuhn) is the transfer of energy as EM waves.

In a vacuum, all EM waves move at the same speed: 300,000,000 m/s, called the speed of light. That's fast enough to circle Earth more than seven times in one second!

Although light and other EM waves do not need a medium, they can travel through many materials. EM waves travel more slowly in a medium such as air or glass than in a vacuum.

Active Reading

5 Identify Underline what produces EM waves.

6 Synthesize Why do we see lightning before we hear the accompanying thunder?

_____
_____
_____
_____

Visualize It!

7 Label Mark and label the wavelength and amplitude of the disturbances in the fields.

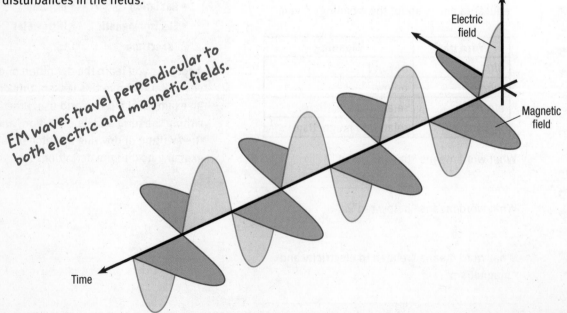

EM waves travel perpendicular to both electric and magnetic fields.

Electric field

Magnetic field

Time

The color with the shortest wavelengths is violet. Violet light has the highest frequencies.

The color with the longest wavelengths is red. Red light has the lowest frequencies.

What determines the color of light?

Light comes in many colors, from red to violet. But what is different about each color of light? Like all waves, light has wavelengths. Different wavelengths of light are interpreted by our eyes as different colors. The shortest wavelengths are seen as violet. The longest wavelengths are seen as red. Even the longest wavelengths we can see are still very small—less than one ten-thousandth of a centimeter.

White light is what we perceive when we see all the wavelengths of light at once, in equal proportions. A prism can split white light into its component colors, separating the colors by wavelength. The various wavelengths of light can also be combined to produce white light.

Our eyes only register three color ranges of light, called the primary colors—red, green, and blue. All other colors we see are a mixture of these three colors. A television or computer screen works by sending signals to make small dots, called pixels, give off red, green, and blue light.

Visualize It!

8 Arrange List the colors of the spectrum in order of increasing wavelength.

_____

_____

_____

_____

_____

_____

Red, green, and blue light combine to appear white.

9 Select What combination of primary colors do we perceive as yellow?

_____

_____

Invisible Colors

What are the parts of the EM spectrum?

EM waves are measured by frequency or by wavelength. The light waves we see are EM waves. However, visible light represents only a very small part of the range of frequencies (or wavelengths) that an EM wave can have. This range is called the **electromagnetic (EM) spectrum**. These other EM waves are the same type of wave as the light we're used to. They're just different frequencies.

Two parts of the spectrum are close to visible light. **Infrared**, or IR, light has slightly longer wavelengths than red light. **Ultraviolet**, or UV, light has slightly shorter wavelengths than violet light.

The Electromagnetic Spectrum

Microwaves
Despite their name, microwaves are not the shortest EM waves. Besides heating food, microwaves are used by cellular phones.

Infrared Light
Infrared means "below red." The amount of infrared light an object gives off depends on its temperature. Below, colors indicate different amounts of infrared light.

17,8°C
0
-20
-40
-60
-74,4°C

Radio Waves
Radio waves have the longest wavelengths. They are used to broadcast signals for radios, televisions, alarm systems, and other devices.

Frequency in hertz (1 hertz = 1 cycle/second)

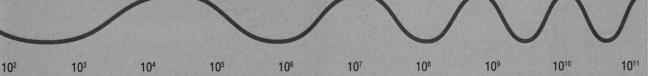

| 10^2 | 10^3 | 10^4 | 10^5 | 10^6 | 10^7 | 10^8 | 10^9 | 10^{10} | 10^{11} |

Radio Waves

Microwaves

© Houghton Mifflin Harcourt Publishing Company • Image Credits: (t) ©Bjorn Rorslett/Photo Researchers, Inc.; (ml) ©Wiskerke/Alamy; (mc) ©Steve Wisbauer/Photodisc/Getty Images; (mr) ©Nutscode/T Service/Photo Researchers, Inc.

The inner part of these flowers reflects UV light differently than the outer part. A bee's eyes are sensitive to UV light, and the bee can see the difference. However, human eyes cannot detect UV light. Our eyes can detect yellow light, and the center and edges of the flower reflect yellow light equally, so we see an all-yellow flower.

Human eyes see the flowers as entirely yellow.

A bee's eyes see a pattern in UV light.

Think Outside the Book

10 Incorporate The flower shows designs that are visible to bees, which can see light in the ultraviolet range. Research and explain how this adaptation leads to a symbiotic relationship between the flowers and bees.

Visible Light
Visible light is all the colors of the EM spectrum we can see. It is the narrowest part of the EM spectrum.

Ultraviolet Light
Ultraviolet means "beyond violet." Some animals can see ultraviolet light.

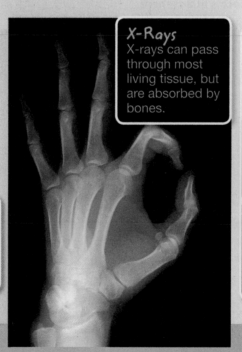

X-Rays
X-rays can pass through most living tissue, but are absorbed by bones.

Gamma Rays
Gamma rays can be used to treat illnesses and in making medical images.

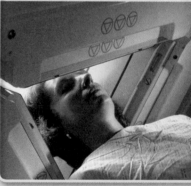

| 10^{12} | 10^{13} | 10^{14} | 10^{15} | 10^{16} | 10^{17} | 10^{18} | 10^{19} | 10^{20} |

Infrared Light   **Ultraviolet Light**   **Gamma Rays**

Visible Light   **X-Rays**

© Houghton Mifflin Harcourt Publishing Company • Image Credits: (t) ©Bjorn Rorslett/Photo Researchers, Inc.; (mlc) ©Jim Wehtje/Photodisc/Getty Images; (mr) ©James King-Holmes/Photo Researchers, Inc.

Star Light,

How much of the sun's energy reaches us?

The sun gives off huge amounts of energy in the form of EM radiation. More of this energy is in the narrow visible light range than any other part of the spectrum, but the sun gives off some radiation in every part of the spectrum.

 **Active Reading** 11 **Identify** What prevents most of the sun's gamma rays from reaching us?

_____

Visualize It!

The illustration shows how far down each part of the EM spectrum penetrates Earth's atmosphere.

The Earth Shields Us from Some EM Radiation

Between the sun and us lies Earth's atmosphere. In order for us to see anything, some of the sun's light must make it through the atmosphere. However, not all wavelengths of light penetrate the atmosphere equally. The atmosphere blocks most of the higher-frequency radiation like x-rays and gamma rays from reaching us at the ground level, while allowing most of the visible light to reach us. There is a "window" of radio frequencies that are barely blocked at all, and this is why the most powerful ground-based telescopes are radio telescopes.

Visible

Radio   Microwave   Infrared ↓ Ultraviolet   X-rays   Gamma rays

Radio and visible light penetrate all the way to the ground. Most ultraviolet light is blocked high in the atmosphere.

12 Apply Why do we keep some telescopes in space?

_____

_____

_____

_____

Star Bright

13 Hypothesize Why might it be less dangerous to wear no sunglasses than to wear sunglasses that do not block UV light?

_____

_____

_____

_____

Astronauts need extra protection from EM radiation in space.

We Shield Ourselves from Some Radiation

The atmosphere blocks much of the sun's radiation, but not all. Some EM radiation can be dangerous to humans, so we take extra steps to protect ourselves. Receiving too much ultraviolet (UV) radiation can cause sunburn, skin cancer, or damage to the eyes, so we wear sunscreen and wear UV-blocking sunglasses to protect ourselves from the UV light that passes through the atmosphere. Hats, long-sleeved shirts, and long pants can protect us, too.

We need this protection even on overcast days because UV light can travel through clouds. Even scientists in Antarctica, one of the coldest places on Earth, need to wear sunglasses, because fresh snow reflects about 80% of UV light back up where it might strike their eyes.

Outer space is often thought of as being cold, but despite this, one of the biggest dangers to astronauts is from overheating! Outside of Earth's protective atmosphere, the level of dangerous EM radiation is much higher. And, in the vacuum of space, it's much harder to dispose of any energy, because there's no surrounding matter (like air) to absorb the extra energy. This is one reason why astronauts' helmets have a thin layer of pure gold. This highly reflective gold layer reflects unwanted EM radiation away.

Frequency Asked Questions

How much energy does EM radiation have?

What makes some EM waves safe, and some dangerous? The answer is that different frequencies of EM waves carry different amounts of energy.

Higher Frequency Means More Energy

The energy of an EM wave depends on its frequency. High-frequency, short-wavelength EM waves have more energy than low-frequency, long-wavelength waves.

More Energy Means More Dangerous

A high-frequency EM wave carries a lot of energy, so it has the possibility of damaging living tissue. But a low-frequency wave carries much less energy, and is safer. This is why radio waves (which have the lowest frequencies) are used so often, such as in walkie-talkies and baby monitors. In contrast, UV light causes sunburn unless you have protection, and when working with even higher-energy waves like x-rays, special precautions must be taken, such as wearing a lead apron to block most of the rays.

> **Think Outside the Book**
>
> 15 **Apply** On a separate sheet of paper, write a short story where the main character needs protection from two different kinds of EM radiation.

Active Reading 14 **Conclude** What kind of EM waves are most dangerous to humans?

Radio waves pass through humans safely.

UV waves can cause damage to living tissue.

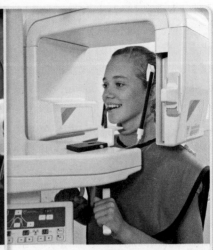

X-rays require extra safety.

Fire in the Sky

The sun constantly streams out charged particles. Earth has a strong magnetic field. When particles from the sun strike Earth, the magnetic field funnels them together, accelerating them. When these particles collide with the atmosphere, they give off electromagnetic radiation in the form of light, and near the poles where they usually come together, a beautiful display called an *aurora* (uh•RAWR•uh) sometimes lights up the sky.

Winds of Change

The stream of electrically charged particles from the sun is called the *solar wind*.

What a Gas!

An aurora produced by nitrogen atoms may have a blue or red color, while one produced by oxygen atoms is green or brownish-red.

Pole Position

At the North Pole, this phenomenon is called the *aurora borealis* (uh•RAWR•uh bawr•ee•AL•is), or northern lights. At the south pole, is it called the *aurora australis* (uh•RAWR•uh aw•STRAY•lis), or southern lights.

Extend

Inquiry

16 Relate Which color of aurora gives off higher-energy light, green or red?

17 Explain Why don't we see auroras on the moon?

18 Hypothesize Based on what you have learned about auroras, do you think auroras occur on other planets? Why or why not?

Visual Summary

To complete this summary, fill in the blanks with the correct word or phrase. Then use the key below to check your answers. You can use this page to review the main concepts of the lesson.

The Electromagnetic Spectrum

Different wavelengths of light appear as different colors.

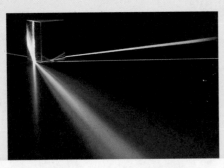

19 The color of the longest visible wavelength is _____

20 The color of the shortest visible wavelength is _____

Higher-frequency waves carry more energy. This makes them more dangerous.

21 The energy of an electromagnetic (EM) wave is proportional to its _____

EM waves exist along a spectrum.

22 The waves with the longest wavelengths are _____ waves.

23 The waves with the shortest wavelengths are _____

10^0 10^{19}

Radio Waves   **Gamma Rays**

Answers: 19 red; 20 violet; 21 frequency; 22 radio; 23 gamma rays

24 Synthesize Suppose you are designing a device to transmit information without wires. What part of the EM spectrum will your device use, and why?

Lesson Review

Vocabulary

Fill in the blanks with the terms that best complete the following sentences.

1 The transfer of energy as electromagnetic waves is called _____

2 The full range of wavelengths of EM waves is called the _____

_____

3 _____ radiation lies at frequencies just below the frequencies of visible light.

Key Concepts

4 Describe What is an electromagnetic wave?

_____

_____

_____

5 Organize What are the highest-frequency and lowest-frequency parts of the EM spectrum?

_____

_____

_____

6 Compare How fast do different parts of the EM spectrum travel in a vacuum?

_____

_____

_____

Suppose you like to listen to two different radio stations. The opera station broadcasts at 90.5 MHz and the rock and roll station broadcasts at 107.1 MHz.

7 Apply Which station's signal has waves with longer wavelengths?

_____

8 Apply Which station's signal has waves with higher energy?

_____

Use the graph to answer the following questions.

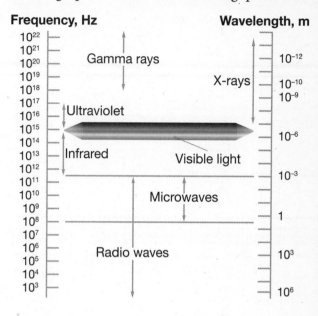

9 Classify How would you classify an EM wave with a frequency of 10^7 Hz?

_____

10 Classify How would you classify an EM wave with a wavelength of 10^{-12} m?

_____

11 Apply What is white light?

_____

_____

Critical Thinking

12 Recommend If you wanted to detect x-rays coming from the sun, where would you place the detector? Why?

_____

_____

_____

_____

_____

My Notes

Interactions of Light

ESSENTIAL QUESTION

How does light interact with matter?

By the end of this lesson, you should be able to explain how light and matter can interact.

These windows allow different colors of light to pass through. The colorful pattern is then reflected off the floor inside.

Lesson Labs

Quick Labs
- Why is the Sky Blue?
- Refraction with Water

Exploration Lab
- Comparing Colors of Objects in Different Colors of Light

Engage Your Brain

1 Predict Check T or F to show whether you think each statement is true or false.

T   F

☐ ☐ Light cannot pass through solid matter.

☐ ☐ A white surface absorbs every color of light.

☐ ☐ Light always moves at the same speed.

2 Identify Unscramble the letters below to find words about interactions between light and matter. Write your words on the blank lines.

OCRLO   _____

RIORMR   _____

NABORIW   _____

TTRACSE   _____

CENFOLRETI   _____

Active Reading

3 Synthesize You can often define an unknown word if you know the meaning of its word parts. Use the word parts and sentence below to make an educated guess about the meanings of the words *transmit*, *transparent*, and *translucent*.

Word part	Meaning
trans-	through
-mit	send
-par	show
-luc	light

transmit: _____

_____

transparent: _____

_____

translucent: _____

_____

Vocabulary Terms

- transparent
- translucent
- opaque
- absorption
- reflection
- refraction
- scattering

4 Apply As you learn the definition of each vocabulary term in this lesson, create your own definition or sketch to help you remember the meaning of the term.

Shedding Light

How can matter interact with light?

Interactions between light and matter produce many common but spectacular effects, such as color, reflections, and rainbows. Three forms of interaction play an especially important role in how people see light.

Matter Can Transmit Light

Recall that light and other electromagnetic waves can travel through empty space. When light encounters a material, it can be passed through the material, or transmitted. The medium can transmit all, some, or none of the light.

Matter that transmits light is **transparent** (tranz•PAHR•uhnt). Air, water, and some types of glass are transparent materials. Objects can be seen clearly through transparent materials.

Translucent (tranz•LOO•suhnt) materials transmit light but do not let the light travel straight through. The light is scattered into many different directions. As a result, you can see light through translucent materials, but objects seen through a translucent material look distorted or fuzzy. Frosted glass, some lamp shades, and tissue paper are examples of translucent materials.

Objects can be seen clearly through transparent glass.

Objects look distorted when seen through translucent glass.

📖 **Active Reading**

5 Identify As you read, underline three words that describe how well matter transmits light.

Think Outside the Book

6 Discuss Write a short story in which it is important that a piece of glass is translucent or transparent.

on the Matter

Matter Can Absorb Light

Opaque (oh•PAYK) materials do not let any light pass through them. Instead, they reflect light, absorb light, or both. Many materials, such as wood, brick, or metal, are opaque. When light enters a material but does not leave it, the light is absorbed. **Absorption** is the transfer of light energy to matter.

The shirt at right absorbs the light that falls on it, and so the shirt is opaque. However, absorption is not the only way an object can be opaque.

The shirt is opaque, because light does not pass through it. We can't see the table underneath.

> **Visualize It!**

7 Explain Is the table in the photo at right transparent, translucent, or opaque? Explain how you know.

_____

_____

_____

Matter Can Reflect Light

You see an object only when light from the object enters your eye. However, most objects do not give off, or emit, light. Instead, light bounces off the object's surface. The bouncing of light off a surface is called **reflection**.

Most objects have a surface that is at least slightly rough. When light strikes a rough surface, such as wood or cloth, the light reflects in many different directions. Some of the reflected light reaches your eyes, and you see the object.

Light bounces at an angle equal to the angle at which it hit the surface. When light strikes a smooth or shiny surface such as a mirror, it reflects in a uniform way. As a result, a mirror produces an image. Light from a lamp might be reflected by your skin, then be reflected by a mirror, and then enter your eye. You look at the mirror and see yourself.

> **Visualize It!**

8 Identify What is the difference between the way light interacts with the shirt above and the way light interacts with the mirror at right?

_____

_____

_____

Light is reflected by the girl's face and by the mirror.

Color Me Impressed!

What determines the color of objects we see?

Visible light includes a range of colors. Light that includes all colors is called white light. When white light strikes an object, the object can transmit some or all of the colors of light, reflect some or all of the colors, and absorb some or all of the colors.

The Light Reflected or Absorbed

The perceived color of an object is determined by the colors of light reflected by the object. For example, a frog's skin absorbs most colors of light, but reflects most of the green light. When you look in the direction of the frog, the green light enters your eyes, so the frog appears green.

An object that reflects every color appears white. An object that absorbs every color appears black.

> **Think Outside the Book**
>
> **9 Diagram** Use colored pencils, crayons, or markers to draw light shining on an object. Draw arrows showing the colors of incoming light and arrows showing which colors are reflected.

The frog's body is green because it reflects green light while absorbing other colors of light.

The Light Transmitted

The color of a transparent or translucent object works differently than it does for opaque objects. Some materials may absorb some colors but let other colors pass through. Green plastic, for example, does not appear green because it reflects green light, but rather, because it transmits green light while absorbing other colors of light. When you look toward a bottle made of green plastic, the transmitted green light reaches your eyes. Therefore, the bottle looks green.

Some matter can absorb visible light but let other kinds of electromagnetic waves pass through. For example, radio waves can easily pass through walls that are opaque to visible light. X-rays pass through skin and muscle, but are stopped by denser bone.

The bottle is green because it allows green light to pass through while absorbing other colors of light.

The Available Light

Sometimes the perceived color of an object depends on the light available in the area. You may have been in a room with a red light bulb. The glass around the bulb filters out all colors except red, plus some orange and yellow. An object that reflects red light would still appear red under such a light bulb. But an object that absorbed all red, orange, and yellow light would appear gray or black. We can't see colors of light that aren't there to be reflected to our eyes!

Filtered Light

Below, the light from the bulb is being filtered before shining on a frog.

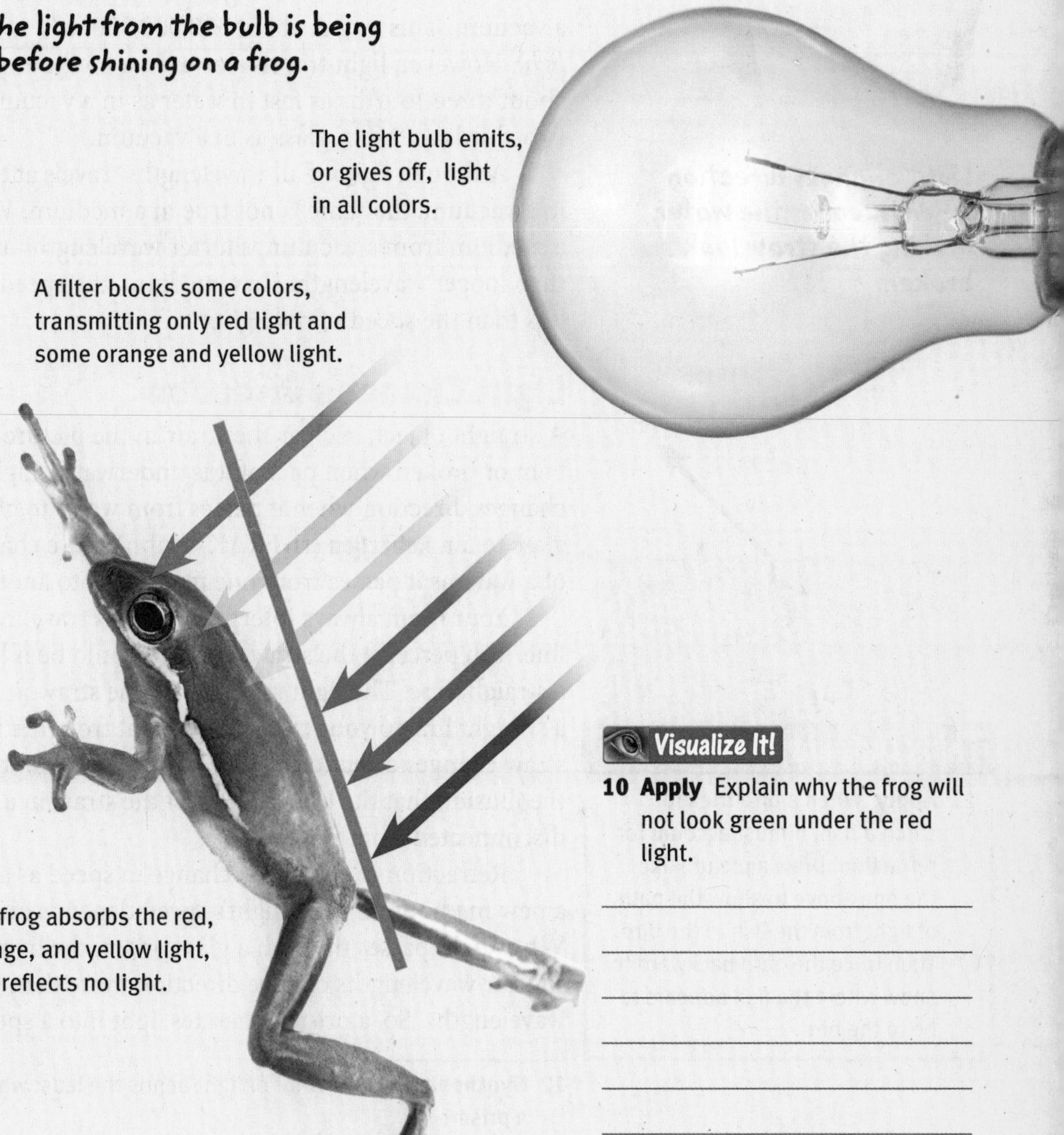

The light bulb emits, or gives off, light in all colors.

A filter blocks some colors, transmitting only red light and some orange and yellow light.

The frog absorbs the red, orange, and yellow light, and reflects no light.

👁 Visualize It!

10 Apply Explain why the frog will not look green under the red light.

_____

_____

_____

_____

_____

_____

Light changes direction when it leaves the water, making the straw look broken.

What happens when light waves interact with matter?

You have already learned that light can pass through a transparent medium. But when light waves pass through a medium, the medium can change properties of the light.

Light Slows When It Passes Through Matter

You may have learned that light always travels at the same speed in a vacuum. This speed, about 300,000,000 m/s, is called the *speed of light*. However, light travels slower in a medium. Light travels only about three-fourths as fast in water as in a vacuum, and only about two-thirds as fast in glass as in a vacuum.

Although light of all wavelengths travels at the same speed in a vacuum, the same is not true in a medium. When light enters a medium from a vacuum, shorter wavelengths are slowed more than longer wavelengths. In a medium, the speed of violet light is less than the speed of red light.

Light Changes Direction

A straight object, such as the straw in the picture above, looks bent or broken when part of it is underwater. Light from the straw changes direction when it passes from water to glass and from glass to air. **Refraction** (ri•FRAK•shuhn) is the change in direction of a wave as it passes from one medium into another at an angle.

Your brain always interprets light as traveling in a straight line. You perceive the straw where it would be if light traveled in a straight line. The light reflected by the straw in air does travel in a straight line to your eye. But the light from the lower part of the straw changes direction when it passes into air. It refracts, causing the illusion that the bottom part of the straw in a water glass is disconnected from the top part.

Refraction is due to the change in speed as a wave enters a new medium. In glass, light's speed depends on wavelength. When light passes through a glass prism, the light waves with shorter wavelengths change direction more than waves with longer wavelengths. So, a prism separates light into a spectrum of colors.

Think Outside the Book

11 Apply When a bird tries to catch a fish, it must account for refraction. Draw a picture like the one above to show the path of light from the fish to the bird. Then trace the path backward to show where the fish appears to be to the bird.

12 Synthesize Which color of light bends the least when passing through a prism?

_____

Light Scatters

You don't see a beam of light shining through clear air. But if the beam of light shines through fog, some of the light is sent in many different directions. Some enters your eye, and you see the beam. **Scattering** occurs when light is sent in many directions as it passes through a medium. Dust and other small particles can scatter light.

The color of the sky is due to scattered light. Particles of air scatter short wavelengths—blue and violet light—more than long wavelengths. As sunlight passes through air, blue light is scattered first. The blue light appears to come from all directions, and so the sky appears blue. When the sun is near the horizon in the sky, sunlight passes through more of the atmosphere. As the light passes through more and more air, almost all light of short wavelengths is scattered. Only the longest wavelengths are left. The sun and the sky appear yellow, orange, or red.

Active Reading

13 Identify What color of light is scattered most easily by the atmosphere?

_____

We can see the light beam coming out of the lighthouse because the fog scatters the light.

In the diagram below, the red lines represent paths of light from the sun. The black brackets show the amount of atmosphere the light must pass through to reach our eyes.

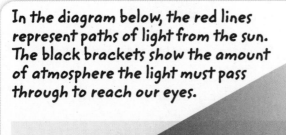

In the evening, sunlight travels through a lot of air. The blue light scatters, leaving only redder light.

The daytime sky appears blue because air scatters blue light more than it does other colors.

Not to scale

Visual Summary

To complete this summary, circle the correct word to complete each statement. Then, use the key below to check your answers. You can use this page to review the main concepts of the lesson.

Interactions of Light and Matter

Matter can transmit, reflect, or absorb light.

14 Matter that transmits no light is (transparent/translucent/opaque).

A transparent medium can bend, scatter, or change the speed of light.

16 The bending of light is called (reflection/refraction/scattering).

The color of an object depends on what colors of light it reflects or transmits.

15 A frog in white light appears green because it (reflects/absorbs/transmits) green light and (reflects/absorbs/transmits) other colors of light.

17 Synthesize Suppose you are looking at a yellow fish in a fish tank. The tank is next to a window. Describe the path that light takes in order for you to see the fish, starting at the sun and ending at your eyes.

Lesson Review

Vocabulary

Fill in the blank with the term that best completes the following sentences.

1 An object appears fuzzy when seen through a(n) _____ material.

2 A(n) _____ material lets light pass through freely.

3 The bouncing of light off a surface is called _____

4 The bending of light when it changes media is called _____

5 _____ occurs when light changes direction after colliding with particles of matter.

Key Concepts

6 Identify For each picture below, identify the material enclosing the sandwich as transparent, translucent, or opaque.

a. _____

b. _____

c. _____

d. _____

7 Identify Which material in the pictures above reflects the most light?

_____

8 Identify Which material in the pictures above absorbs the most light?

_____

Critical Thinking

9 Infer Is a mirror's surface transparent, translucent, or opaque? How do you know?

_____
_____
_____
_____
_____

10 Apply Why does a black asphalt road become hotter than a white cement sidewalk in the same amount of sunlight?

_____
_____
_____
_____
_____

11 Explain Why is the sky blue?

_____
_____
_____
_____
_____
_____
_____
_____

12 Explain Red, green, and blue light rays each enter a drop of water from the same direction. Which light ray's path through the drop will bend the most, and which will bend the least? Why?

_____
_____
_____
_____

My Notes

Mirrors and Lenses

ESSENTIAL QUESTION

How do mirrors and lenses work?

By the end of this lesson, you should be able to describe ways that lenses and mirrors form images.

The curves on this funhouse mirror produce distorted images of the people and objects nearby.

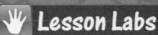 **Lesson Labs**

Quick Labs
• Mirror Images
• Spoon Images

S.T.E.M. Lab
• Light Maze

 Engage Your Brain

1 Infer Why do you think the word *ambulance* is printed backwards on the front of this emergency vehicle?

_____

_____

_____

_____

2 Predict If your hair is usually parted on the left side, how will it appear in your bathroom mirror?

_____

_____

 Active Reading

3 Apply Use context clues to write your own definitions for the words *image* and *virtual*.

Example sentence:
When I see myself in a funhouse mirror, my <u>image</u> is distorted and I look weird.

image:

_____

_____

_____

Example sentence:
Some mirrors produce a <u>virtual</u> image; other mirrors produce a real image.

virtual:

_____

_____

Vocabulary Terms

• virtual image   • convex
• concave   • diverge
• converge   • lens
• real image

4 Apply As you learn the definition of each vocabulary term in this lesson, create your own definition or sketch to help you remember the meaning of the term.

Mirror Image

How do mirrors form images?

Light waves travel from their source in all directions. If you could trace the path of one light wave, you would find that it is a straight line. If a light wave hits an object, it may be reflected, or bounce off. Most objects have rough surfaces that reflect light in many different directions. A very smooth surface, such as a mirror, reflects light in a uniform way. Look at the illustrations below. The light from the flashlight hits the mirror at an angle of 40° from an imaginary line perpendicular to the mirror's surface. This imaginary line is called the *normal*. Notice that the angle at which light hits the surface is equal to the angle at which the light is reflected from the surface. This is called the *law of reflection*.

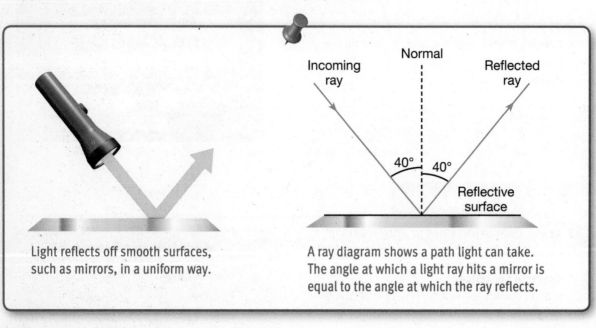

Light reflects off smooth surfaces, such as mirrors, in a uniform way.

A ray diagram shows a path light can take. The angle at which a light ray hits a mirror is equal to the angle at which the ray reflects.

 **Do the Math** You Try It

5 Analyze Use a protractor to find the angles at which the light hits the mirror and is reflected from it. Measure from the normal. Write each measurement on the diagram.

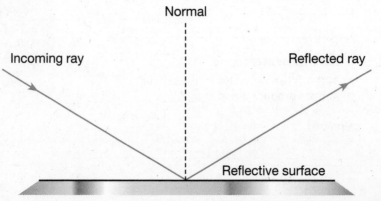

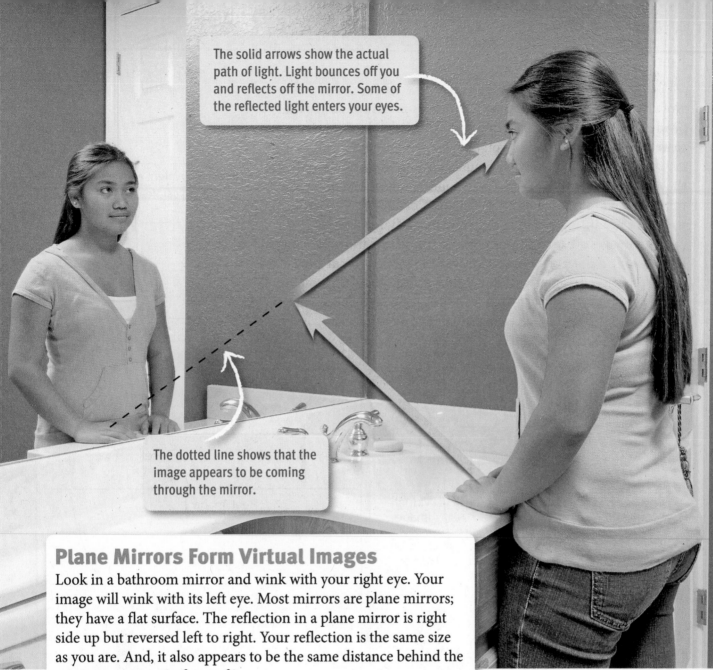

The solid arrows show the actual path of light. Light bounces off you and reflects off the mirror. Some of the reflected light enters your eyes.

The dotted line shows that the image appears to be coming through the mirror.

Plane Mirrors Form Virtual Images

Look in a bathroom mirror and wink with your right eye. Your image will wink with its left eye. Most mirrors are plane mirrors; they have a flat surface. The reflection in a plane mirror is right side up but reversed left to right. Your reflection is the same size as you are. And, it also appears to be the same distance behind the mirror as you are in front of it.

Why does your image seem to be inside the mirror? The picture shows how light is reflected off a plane mirror. When you see reflected light, your brain thinks the light has traveled in a straight line from behind the mirror. In ray diagrams, this type of ray is shown as a dotted line, because it does not represent actual light. Rather, it shows where the light appears to come from. The image formed in a plane mirror is a virtual image. A **virtual image** is an image that appears to come from a place that the light does not actually come from.

Active Reading **6 Apply** What do all plane mirrors have in common?

_____

_____

© Houghton Mifflin Harcourt Publishing Company • Image Credits: ©HMH

Think Outside the Book

7 Identify Walk through your home and list as many examples of plane mirrors as you can find.

Concave Mirrors Form Real or Virtual Images

Not all mirrors are flat. A **concave** mirror is curved inward like the bowl of a spoon. Concave mirrors cause parallel light waves to **converge**, or come together. If you pointed parallel light rays toward the concave mirror below, they would converge at a point called the *focal point*. Or, if you held a light source at that focal point, the mirror would reflect parallel rays of light. Concave mirrors are useful for producing beams of light and magnifying objects.

All images are formed where two or more rays from the same location on an object converge. Concave mirrors can form either virtual images or real images. But, unlike a virtual image, a **real image** is formed where light from an object converges. A real image can be projected onto a screen; a virtual image cannot.

8 Infer How might concave mirrors be used in car headlights?

_____

_____

_____

_____

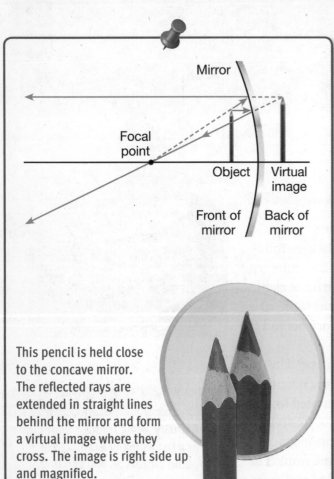

This pencil is held close to the concave mirror. The reflected rays are extended in straight lines behind the mirror and form a virtual image where they cross. The image is right side up and magnified.

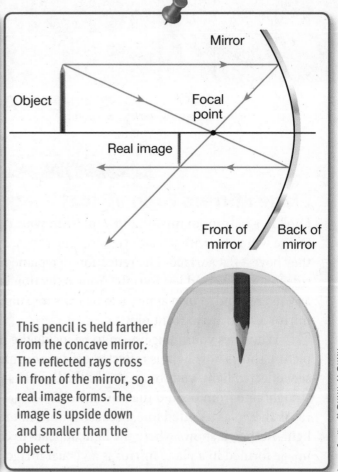

This pencil is held farther from the concave mirror. The reflected rays cross in front of the mirror, so a real image forms. The image is upside down and smaller than the object.

Visualize It! Inquiry

9 Predict What would happen to the size of the image if the green pencil were moved farther away from the mirror? If possible, test your prediction using the inside of a spoon as a mirror.

_____

Convex Mirrors Form Virtual Images

A **convex** mirror curves outward like the back of a spoon. Convex mirrors cause a beam of light to **diverge**, or spread apart, as if it came from a focal point behind the mirror. If you look at your reflection in the back of a spoon, you will notice that your image is right side up and small. You may also be able to see the floor or ceiling around you.

All images formed by convex mirrors are virtual, right side up, and small. Convex mirrors are useful because they make small images of large areas. They are used for security in stores and factories. Many cars, buses, and trucks use convex side mirrors so the driver can see more of the surrounding area.

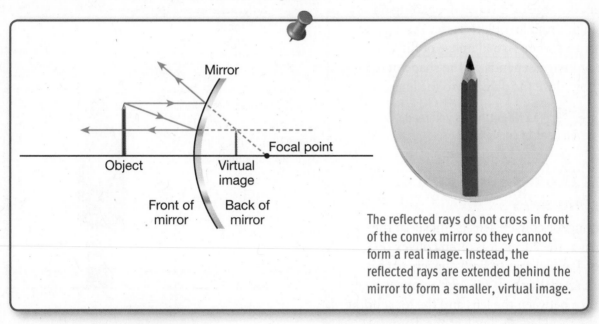

The reflected rays do not cross in front of the convex mirror so they cannot form a real image. Instead, the reflected rays are extended behind the mirror to form a smaller, virtual image.

Visualize It!

10 Diagram In the space below, draw a ray diagram to represent what you might see in the gazing ball on the left.

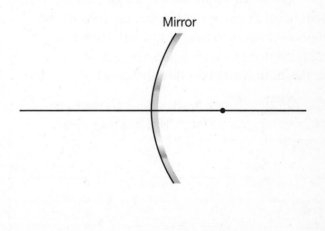

Mirror

Under a Lens

How do lenses form images?

A **lens** is a clear optical tool that refracts light. Refraction occurs when a light wave changes speed as it passes from one medium to another. The change in speed makes the light waves bend and either converge or diverge, depending on the lens. Light from an object passes through a lens to form a real or virtual image of the object. The type of image depends on the shape of the lens and how close the object is to the lens.

Active Reading 11 **Identify** As you read, underline seven uses of convex lenses.

Convex Lenses Form Real or Virtual Images

A converging, or convex, lens is thicker at the center than at the edges. It is often convex on both sides. Parallel rays of light converge at a focal point after they pass through a convex lens. The distance between the lens and the focal point is called the focal length. Look at the diagrams on the right. The lens shown in the top diagram is thicker in the center and has a focal length that is longer than the lens shown in the bottom diagram. Also notice that the pencil shown in the top diagram is held closer to the lens than the pencil shown in the bottom diagram.

Convex lenses are used to magnify or to focus light. They are used in magnifying glasses, telescopes, microscopes, binoculars, cameras, and projectors. Convex lenses are used in eyeglasses to correct for farsightedness.

Active Reading 12 **Provide** What are two factors that affect how much a magnifying lens magnifies an object?

_____

_____

_____

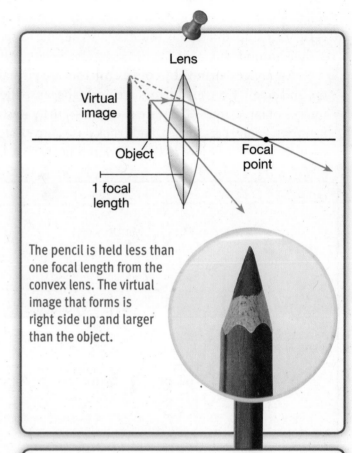

The pencil is held less than one focal length from the convex lens. The virtual image that forms is right side up and larger than the object.

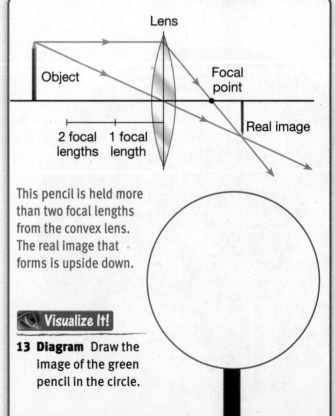

This pencil is held more than two focal lengths from the convex lens. The real image that forms is upside down.

Visualize It!

13 **Diagram** Draw the image of the green pencil in the circle.

Concave Lenses Form Virtual Images

A diverging, or concave, lens is thinner at the center than at the edges. It is often concave on both sides. Light that passes through a concave lens is refracted outward as if from the focal point.

Because they are refracted away from each other, parallel light waves passing through a concave lens do not meet. The image formed is a virtual image. It is right side up and smaller than the object. In concave lenses, the distance between the object and the lens does not make a difference in the type of image that is formed.

Diverging lenses are used to spread light, often in combination with other lenses in telescopes and binoculars. They are also used in eyeglasses to correct for nearsightedness.

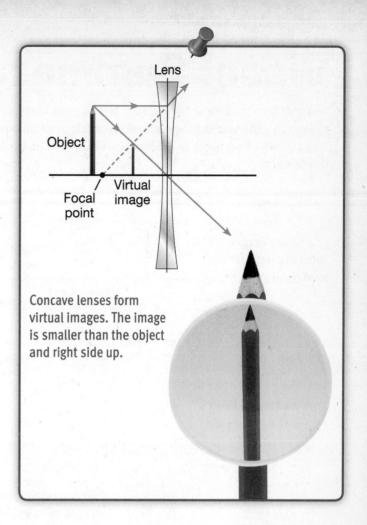

Concave lenses form virtual images. The image is smaller than the object and right side up.

Review: Mirrors and Lenses

14 **Summarize** Use what you know about mirrors and lenses to write either *concave* or *convex* in the *Optical device* column. Provide a real-world example for each kind of mirror and lens.

Virtual or real?	Orientation of image	Size of image in relation to object	Optical device	Real-world example
virtual	right side up	larger	_____ lens	
real	upside down	smaller	_____ mirror	
virtual	right side up	smaller	_____ lens	
virtual	right side up	larger	_____ mirror	
real	upside down	smaller	_____ lens	
virtual	right side up	smaller	_____ mirror	

Visual Summary

To complete this summary, circle the correct word or phrase. Then, use the key below to check your answers. You can use this page to review the main concepts of the lesson.

Mirrors and Lenses

Concave mirrors form either real or virtual images.

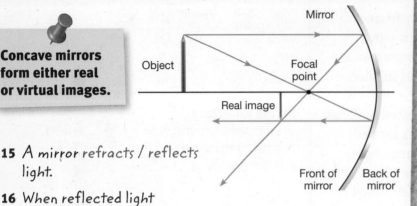

15 A mirror refracts / reflects light.

16 When reflected light converges, a real / virtual image is formed.

Concave lenses produce only virtual images.

19 A concave lens is thinner / thicker in the center than at the edges.

20 A concave lens produces a magnified / smaller image.

Convex mirrors form virtual images.

17 A convex mirror curves inward / outward.

18 Light does / does not pass through a virtual image.

Convex lenses produce real or virtual images.

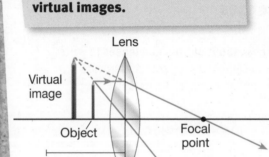

21 A convex lens causes parallel rays of light to spread out / converge.

22 The image produced by a convex lens when the object is close to the lens is real / virtual.

Answers: 15 reflects; 16 real; 17 outward; 18 does not; 19 thinner; 20 smaller; 21 converge; 22 virtual

---

23 **Explain** Using what you know about images and lenses, explain why projectors use convex instead of concave lenses.

Lesson Review

Vocabulary

Draw a line to connect the following terms to their definitions.

1 converge

2 diverge

3 convex

4 concave

5 real image

6 virtual image

A reflected or refracted light converges

B thick center and thin edges

C reflected or refracted light does not cross

D spread apart

E bring together

F thin center and thick edges

Key Concepts

7 Classify What do you see when you look at yourself in a plane mirror?

A a real image that appears to be inside the mirror

B a real image that appears to be in front of the mirror

C a virtual image that appears to be inside the mirror

D a virtual image that appears to be in front of the mirror

8 Distinguish What determines whether a real or a virtual image is formed from a concave mirror?

_____

_____

_____

9 Explain How does a concave lens affect rays of light?

_____

_____

10 Apply What can you use a convex lens to do when you hold it close to an object?

_____

_____

Critical Thinking

11 Classify How can you use a screen to determine whether an image is real or virtual?

_____

_____

_____

12 Apply What kind of mirror do you think is used in the side-view mirror of cars? Explain.

_____

_____

_____

_____

13 Justify Why can a ray be used to represent light in a ray diagram?

A Light waves are electromagnetic waves.

B Light waves spread out in all directions.

C Light waves travel in straight lines.

D Light waves can be reflected or refracted.

Use this drawing to answer the following questions.

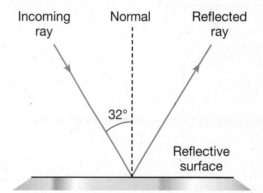

Incoming ray   Normal   Reflected ray

32°

Reflective surface

14 Analyze What is the angle of the reflected ray in the diagram above?

_____

15 Diagram On the diagram, draw the incoming and reflected rays for light hitting the mirror at a 50° angle from the normal.

My Notes

Engineering Design Process

Skills
Identify a need
Conduct research
✓ Brainstorm solutions
✓ Select a solution
Design a prototype
✓ Build a prototype
✓ Test and evaluate
✓ Redesign to improve
✓ Communicate results

Objectives
• Identify different uses of mirrors and lenses.
• Use mirrors and lenses to design and build a periscope.
• Test and evaluate the periscope you built.

Building a Periscope

A *periscope* is a device that uses mirrors and lenses to help people see around obstacles. You might be surprised to learn how many other important technologies benefit from mirrors and lenses.

Early Uses of Mirrors and Lenses

For many centuries, people have used mirrors and lenses to bend light. In ancient times, people used shiny metal to see their reflections and pieces of curved glass to start fires. In the 17th century, scientists began using lenses and mirrors to make telescopes, microscopes, and other devices that helped them make new discoveries.

In 1610, Italian astronomer Galileo used a two-lens telescope to discover Jupiter's moons.

1 Identify List devices that use mirrors, lenses, or a combination of both. Then describe the purpose of each device, and identify whether it uses mirrors, lenses, or both.

Device	Purpose	Mirrors, Lenses, or Both
telescope	magnifies far away objects	both

Lasers

Mirrors bend light by reflecting it in a different direction. Lenses bend light by slowing it as it passes through the lens material. Many modern technologies also take advantage of mirrors and lenses. Devices such as DVD players and barcode scanners operate by using laser light. A *laser* is a device that produces a coherent beam of light of a specific wavelength, or color. Laser light is created in a chamber that has mirrors on each end. A single color of light is produced by reflecting light back and forth between the two mirrors. The distance between the mirrors determines the wavelength of light that is amplified. When the light is of the proper wavelength, it can exit the transparent center of one of the mirrors. Lenses are often found in devices that use laser light. Lenses can focus the laser light in devices such as DVD players.

2 Identify Conduct research about the uses of laser light. What are some objects that use lasers?

_____

_____

_____

This device uses mirrors and lasers to measure the wind speed during an aircraft test. Wind speed is measured as the laser interacts with dust in the wind.

Periscopes

A periscope is another type of device that uses mirrors and lenses. The mirrors in a periscope bend light in order to allow a person to see around obstacles or above water. Most people think of periscopes in submarines, but periscopes are also used to see over walls or around corners, to see out of parade floats, and to see inside pipes or machinery.

Submarine periscopes use lenses and mirrored prisms to allow people to see above the water without surfacing.

 You Try It! ⟶

Now it's your turn to use mirrors and lenses to design and build a periscope.

 # You Try It!

Mirrors are used to bend light, and lenses are used to focus light. Now it's your turn to use mirrors and lenses to design and build a periscope that can see at least six inches above eye level.

You Will Need

✔ cardboard boxes or poster board

✔ cardboard or plastic tubes

✔ lenses

✔ mirrors

✔ scissors

✔ tape

1 Brainstorm Solutions

A You will build a periscope to see things at least six inches above eye level. Brainstorm some ideas about how your periscope will work. Check a box in each row below to get started.

Length of periscope: ☐ 6 inches   ☐ 12 inches   ☐ other _____

Shape of periscope: ☐ tube   ☐ box   ☐ other _____

User will look with: ☐ one eye   ☐ both eyes

Your periscope: ☐ will   ☐ will not   magnify objects

B Once you have decided what your periscope needs to do, look at the materials available to you, and brainstorm how you can build your periscope. Write down the materials you will use and how you will use them.

_____

_____

_____

2 Select a Solution

Choose one of the ideas that you brainstormed. In the space below, draw a sketch of how your prototype periscope will be constructed. Include arrows to show the path of light through your periscope.

③ **Build a Prototype**

Use your materials to assemble the periscope according to your design. Write down the steps you took to assemble the parts.

_____

_____

_____

_____

④ **Test, Evaluate, and Redesign to Improve**

Test your periscope, and fill in the first row of the table below. Make any improvements, and test your periscope again, filling in an additional row of the table for each revised prototype.

Prototype	What I saw through the periscope	Improvements to be made
1		
2		
3		

⑤ **Communicate Results**

Write a paragraph summarizing what you wanted the periscope to do, how you designed and built it, whether the finished periscope worked as planned, and how you made improvements.

_____

_____

_____

_____

_____

_____

_____

Light Waves and Sight

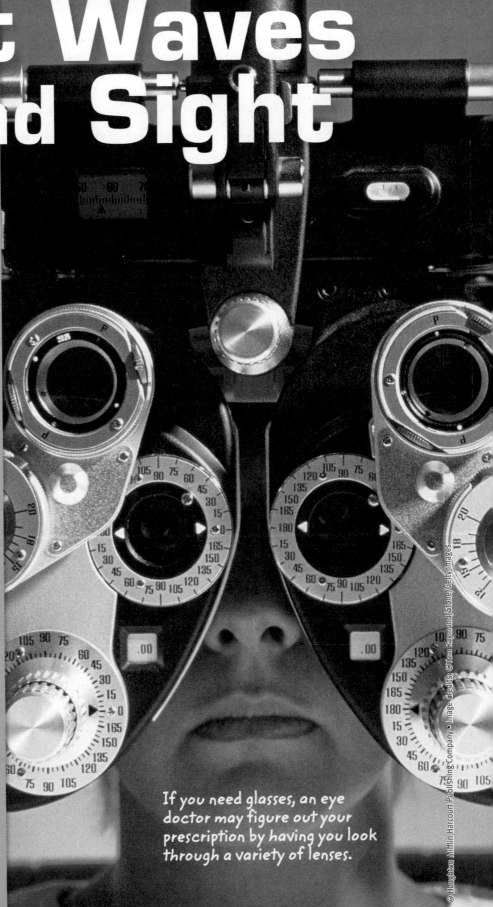

ESSENTIAL QUESTION

How do people see?

By the end of this lesson, you should be able to explain how the eye functions and works with the brain to produce vision.

If you need glasses, an eye doctor may figure out your prescription by having you look through a variety of lenses.

Engage Your Brain

1 Predict Check **T** or **F** to show whether you think each statement is true or false.

T	F	
☐	☐	The shape of your eye can make you farsighted or nearsighted.
☐	☐	One way to correct vision problems is through surgery.
☐	☐	The cornea of your eye controls the amount of light let in.
☐	☐	The brain collects signals from the eyes about an image and flips it right side up.

2 Illustrate Draw and label the parts of the eye that you are familiar with.

Active Reading

3 Apply Many scientific words, such as *focus*, also have everyday meanings. Use context clues to write your own definition for each meaning of the word *focus*.

Example sentence

I need to stop listening to music and <u>focus</u> on getting my homework done.

focus:

_____

_____

Example sentence

A convex lens can be used to <u>focus</u> light rays into a point.

focus:

_____

_____

Vocabulary Terms

- cornea
- retina

4 Apply As you learn the definition of each vocabulary term in this lesson, create your own definition or sketch to help you remember the meaning of the term.

Let's Focus

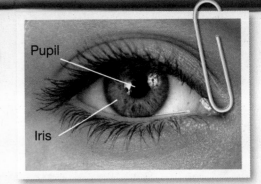

Pupil

Iris

How do people detect and interpret light waves?

How do your eyes and brain work together so that you can see things? You see an object when your eyes detect light and send signals to your brain. Some objects produce their own light, while other objects reflect light. No matter where the light comes from, the light has to enter your eye before you can see anything.

Visualize It!

5 Label After you read, add these labels to the art: cornea, pupil, retina, optic nerve.

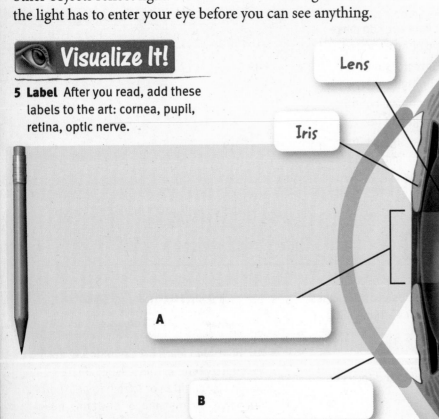

Lens

Iris

A

B

Active Reading **6 Identify** As you read, underline two parts of the eye that refract light.

Light Waves Enter the Eye

Light waves enter the eye through the **cornea**, which is the transparent membrane that forms the front part of the eye. The cornea refracts, or bends, the light so that it passes through the pupil at the center of the iris. The iris changes the size of the pupil to control the amount of light let in. The light refracts again as it enters the lens. Muscles around the lens change its thickness so that objects at different distances can be seen in focus.

An Image Is Focused on the Retina

Images are received by the **retina**, the light-sensitive tissue that lines the inside of the eye. The retina is the part of the eye that detects light and sends signals to the brain. The image is actually focused upside down onto the retina. Two types of cells in the retina detect light—rod cells and cone cells. Rods are very sensitive and can detect even dim light. Cones detect brighter light and colors.

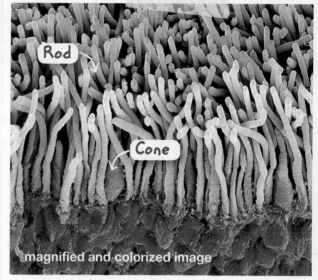

Rod

Cone

magnified and colorized image

C

Image

D

7 Compare Fill in the Venn diagram to compare and contrast rod cells and cone cells.

Rod cells

Cone cells

Both

The Brain Interprets the Signal

The rod and cone cells convert the input they receive into electrical signals. The signals travel to the brain over a bundle of tissue called the *optic nerve*. Different parts of the brain take in these signals and interpret the color, shape, movement, and location of the image. Although the image is sent upside down, the brain understands the image as being right side up. The brain also combines slightly different information from the right and left eyes to produce a sense of distance and depth.

Out of Sight

What are some common vision problems?

Because the eye is complex, there are many things that can affect how well a person's vision works. Common vision problems happen when light is not focused on the retina or when a part of the eye does not work properly.

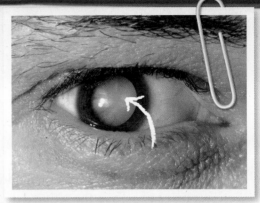

The clouding of an eye lens, called a cataract, interferes with light entering the eye.

Nearsightedness

Nearsightedness happens when a person's eye is too long or their cornea is curved steeply. Nearsighted eyes produce an image in front of the retina rather than on the retina. A nearsighted person can see something clearly only if it is nearby. Faraway objects look blurry.

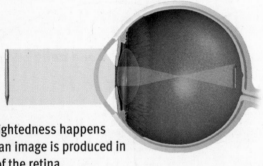

Nearsightedness happens when an image is produced in front of the retina.

Farsightedness

Farsightedness happens when a person's eye is too short or the cornea is not curved enough. Farsighted eyes see distant objects most clearly. Things that are nearby look blurry to a person who is farsighted. People are sometimes born farsighted and grow out of it as they get older.

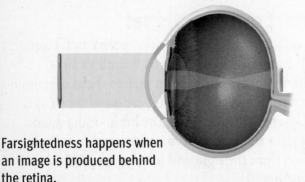

Farsightedness happens when an image is produced behind the retina.

Color Vision Deficiency

About 5% to 8% of men and 0.5% of women in the world have color vision deficiency. This condition is often called color blindness, but very few people cannot see any color. Color vision deficiency happens when the cones in the retina do not work properly. A person who has normal vision can see all colors of visible light. But in some people, the cones respond to the wrong colors. These people see certain colors, such as red and green, as a different color, such as yellow. Color vision deficiency cannot be corrected.

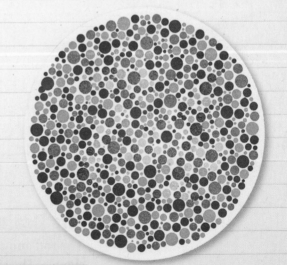

👁 **Visualize It!**

8 Apply About 8% of males and 0.5% of females have red-green color deficiency. If you can see the number hidden in the test pattern above, write it here.

_____

How can vision problems be corrected?

Nearsightedness and farsightedness are commonly corrected with eyeglasses or contact lenses. But lenses are not the only option. These vision problems can also be corrected with laser surgery.

With Corrective Lenses

Nearsightedness can be corrected with a concave lens. Light bends away from the thin center of a concave lens, and the image moves back to the retina. Farsightedness can be corrected with a convex lens. Light bends toward the wide middle of a convex lens, and the image moves forward to the retina.

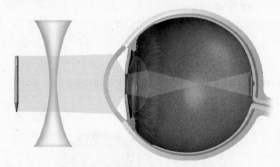

A concave lens placed in front of a nearsighted eye bends the light outward. The lens in the eye can then focus the light on the retina.

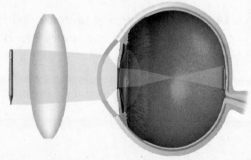

A convex lens placed in front of a farsighted eye focuses the light inward. The lens in the eye can then focus the light on the retina.

👁 **Visualize It!**

9 Synthesize Why are concave lenses, rather than convex lenses, used to treat nearsightedness?

_____

_____

_____

_____

With Contact Lenses or Surgery

Contact lenses correct vision by changing the shape of the cornea. Corrective eye surgery also works by reshaping the patient's cornea. Reshaping the cornea changes how light is focused on the retina. During surgery, a thin flap is folded back from the surface of the eye. The cornea is then reshaped with a laser so the patient gains perfect or nearly perfect vision.

Active Reading **10 State** What part of the eye is changed by vision correction surgery or contact lenses?

_____

_____

Vision correction surgery works by reshaping the front part of the eye.

Think Outside the Book Inquiry

11 Design Build a model that shows how to correct a common vision problem and share the model with your class.

Visual Summary

To complete this summary, choose the word that best completes the sentence. Then use the key below to check your answers. You can use this page to review the main concepts of the lesson.

Light Waves and Sight

Nearsighted eyes produce an image in front of the retina.

13 Concave lenses spread/focus light so that the image is moved back to the retina.

Light reflects off objects and enters the eye through the cornea.

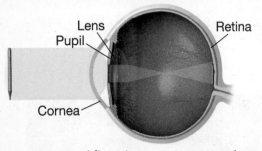

Lens
Pupil
Retina
Cornea

12 The pupil/lens limits how much light enters the eye.

Farsighted eyes produce an image behind the retina.

14 Convex lenses spread/focus light so that the image is moved up to the retina.

Answers: 12 pupil; 13 spread; 14 focus

15 Analyze Why is it important for the lens to be attached to muscles in the eye?

Lesson Review

Vocabulary

Fill in the blank with the term that best completes the following sentences.

1 The _____ is a clear covering on the surface of an eye that focuses light as it enters the eye.

2 The _____ inside the eye further focuses light.

3 Inside the eye, an image is produced on the _____, and signals are sent to the brain.

Key Concepts

4 Distinguish Compare the function of rod cells and cone cells.

_____
_____
_____
_____
_____

5 Explain How does the brain help with vision?

_____
_____
_____
_____

6 Compare How are nearsighted eyes different from eyes with normal vision?

_____
_____
_____
_____

7 Conclude Why can even a small injury to the cornea have a major effect on vision?

_____
_____
_____
_____

Critical Thinking

Use these drawings to answer the following questions.

8 Draw Place an *X* on the top diagram of the eye to show where an image would be in a nearsighted eye.

9 Draw Place an *X* on the bottom diagram of the eye to show where an image would be in a farsighted eye.

10 Predict Which eye's problem could be corrected with a concave lens?

_____

11 Predict Which eye's problem could be corrected by increasing the curve of the cornea?

_____

12 Infer What might happen to a person's sense of depth or distance if they have only one functioning eye?

_____
_____
_____
_____
_____
_____

My Notes

Light Technology

ESSENTIAL QUESTION

How can light be used?

By the end of this lesson, you should be able to apply knowledge of light to describe light-related technologies.

The searchlights on these buildings can be seen from miles away.

Lesson Labs

Quick Labs
• Total Internal Reflection
• Light Technology in Color Monitors

Exploration Lab
• Investigating Artificial Light

Engage Your Brain

1 Predict Check T or F to show whether you think each statement is true or false.

T	F	
☐	☐	Light can be used to perform surgery.
☐	☐	Light cannot be used to transmit sound or data.
☐	☐	Lasers emit light of all frequencies.
☐	☐	Light technology has stayed the same for decades.
☐	☐	Telescopes can use either lenses or mirrors to manipulate light.

2 Describe Do you think this fiber optic lamp is an example of light technology? Explain.

_____

_____

_____

_____

Active Reading

3 Apply Many scientific words, such as *fiber*, also have everyday meanings. Use context clues to write your own definition for each meaning of the word *fiber*.

Example sentence
Clothes can be made of wool <u>fibers</u>.

fiber:

_____

_____

Example sentence
Optical <u>fibers</u> use light to transmit information.

fiber:

_____

_____

Vocabulary Terms

• incandescent light • laser
• fluorescent light • optical fiber
• LED

4 Identify As you read, place a question mark next to any words you don't understand. When you finish reading the lesson, go back and review the text that you marked. If the information is still confusing, consult a classmate or a teacher.

I Can See the LIGHT

What are some ways to produce light?

Throughout history, people have developed different ways of producing light to help see things, store and transfer information, and interact with matter. These are considered light technologies. For example, candles were an early invention that helped people see and work even after the sun went down. We now have a wider variety of technologies that produce and use light.

Incandescent Lights

Visible light produced from a very hot material is **incandescent light** (in•kuhn•DES•uhnt LYT). In a typical incandescent bulb, electric current is passed through a thin wire, called a *filament*, inside the bulb. The filament gets hot enough to *emit*, or give off, visible light. Incandescent bulbs are inefficient in producing light compared with other types of bulbs. Only about 8% of the energy given off by an incandescent light bulb is in the form of light. The rest is in the form of heat.

Fluorescent Lights

Electric current can energize some gases and produce ultraviolet light, which is invisible to humans. **Fluorescent light** (flu•RES•uhnt LYT) is produced when a fluorescent coating inside a bulb converts the ultraviolet light into visible light. About 80% of the energy given off by fluorescent bulbs is in the form of visible light. Fluorescent bulbs last about 10 times longer than incandescent bulbs. The screens of many devices produce light using similar technologies.

6 Compare Fill in the Venn diagram to compare and contrast incandescent and fluorescent light bulbs.

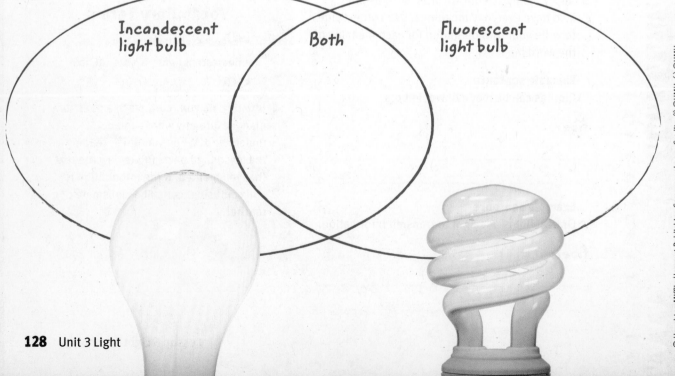

Incandescent light bulb

Both

Fluorescent light bulb

Light-Emitting Diodes

The tiny indicator light on many electronic devices is a *light-emitting diode*, or *LED*. **LEDs** contain solid materials that emit light when energized by an electric current. Unlike other light sources, an LED emits only one color of light. Almost 100% of the energy given off by LEDs is in the form of visible light. This means that LEDs are very efficient and last a long time. Most traffic lights in the United States now use LEDs.

A string of LEDs can provide light for many years.

Lasers

A **laser** is a device that produces intense light of a very small range of wavelengths. Lasers produce light in such a way that causes the light to be more concentrated, or intense, than other types of light. Unlike non-laser light, laser light is *coherent*. When light is coherent, light waves stay together as they travel away from their source. The crests and troughs of coherent light waves are aligned. So the individual waves behave as one wave. The diagram below shows how lasers produce coherent light.

A laser pointer emits a thin, narrow beam of light.

7 Infer What might be an advantage of focusing light into a narrow beam?

_____

_____

_____

How a Helium-Neon Laser Works

A The inside of the laser is filled with helium and neon gases. An electric current in the laser "excites" the atoms of the gases.

B Excited neon atoms release photons of red light. When these photons strike other excited neon atoms, more photons are released that travel together.

C Plane mirrors on both ends of the laser reflect the photons back and forth along the tube.

D Because the photons travel back and forth many times, many more photons are released, and the laser light gets brighter.

E A partial coating on one mirror allows the laser light to escape and form a coherent beam.

Light SPEED

What are some ways light can transfer information?

Some light technologies use light to encode, send, or read signals. For example, a laser inside a CD or DVD player reads the information stored on the disc. Other examples are the bar code scanners in retail stores that record the price of your purchase and TV remote controls that are used to transfer information. Remote controls typically use infrared light.

Infrared Technologies

Infrared radiation is invisible electromagnetic radiation with a wavelength longer than what our eyes can detect. However, several technologies make use of infrared radiation. Some night vision goggles can emit infrared radiation, allowing people to see objects without the help of visible light. Weather satellites can track storms forming at night by taking infrared pictures. Space-based telescopes can determine the temperatures of stars and dust clouds by measuring the infrared radiation coming from them.

Active Reading 8 **Identify** As you read, underline three uses of optical fibers.

Fiber Optic Technologies

A thin, transparent glass thread that transmits light over long distances is an **optical fiber**. A bundle of optical fibers is shown on the left. Transmitting information through telephone cables is the most common use of optical fibers. They are also used to network computers and to allow doctors to see inside patients' bodies without performing major surgery.

Optical fibers are like pipes that carry light. Light stays inside an optical fiber because of *total internal reflection*. Total internal reflection is the complete reflection of light back and forth along the inside surface of the material through which it travels. Light is emitted out the end of the fiber.

An optical fiber is flexible and can transmit light with little loss.

Visualize It!

9 **Diagram** Draw a circle on the fiber optic diagram to show where light is emitted.

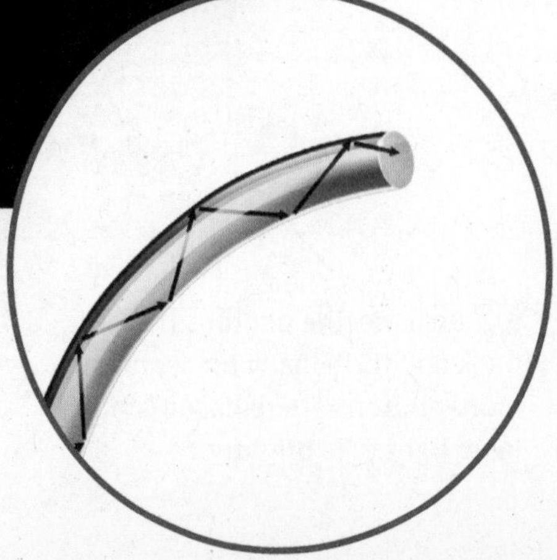

Light traveling through an optical fiber reflects off the sides thousands of times each meter.

© Houghton Mifflin Harcourt Publishing Company • Image Credits: ©Kulka/zefa/Corbis

Satellites in orbit 20,000 km above Earth emit microwaves that are detected by GPS receivers.

Smartphones equipped with GPS receivers can help people navigate a city.

Satellite Technologies

Another technology that uses electromagnetic waves to transmit data is satellite technology. Some satellites are used to send TV, radio, and cell phone data to your home. Weather and government satellites also transmit data using electromagnetic waves.

The Global Positioning System (GPS) is a network of 24 satellites that orbit Earth. These satellites continuously send microwave signals. The signals can be picked up by a GPS receiver on Earth and used to measure positions on Earth's surface. GPS was originally used by the U.S. military. Now, anyone in the world who has a GPS receiver can use the system. Many cars have GPS road maps that help the car's driver navigate to a certain place. Hikers and campers use GPS receivers to find their way in the wilderness.

10 Compare What do infrared technologies, fiber optic technologies, and satellite technologies all have in common?

_____

_____

_____

Light
WORK

A truck with a radar dish can follow storm clouds and gather information about them.

What are some ways light can interact with matter?

Light technologies can make use of the ways light interacts with matter to get information about materials. The light emitted, absorbed, or reflected by objects contains an amazing amount of information about the objects' composition, motion, and temperature. Light technologies, such as lasers, can also be used to produce and control energy to actually change matter.

Doppler Radar

Doppler radar uses light in the form of radio waves to measure weather patterns. Radio waves are sent out toward a weather system. They bounce off of the clouds and back to the transmitter, which captures them for analysis. The frequency of the radio waves changes a small amount, depending on how the weather system is moving. The reflected radio waves are received, and the image is used to make a picture of the entire moving weather system. The speed and intensity of the moving system can be determined.

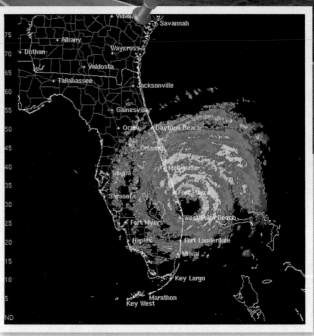

Doppler radar uses light to measure the intensity, location, and movement of a storm system, such as this hurricane. On the radar map, blue is used to show the areas with the lightest rain. Yellow and green represent moderate rain.

Active Reading

11 Identify What form of light does Doppler radar use?

_____

_____

Laser Technologies

The light from lasers can be accurately pointed. The intense energy of the light beam can be used to melt and cut different materials. For example, lasers can be used in manufacturing to cut, weld, and engrave certain metals. Doctors sometimes use lasers for surgery because a laser can be used to make very precise incisions. Lasers are used to shape the cornea of the eye to correct eyesight.

Lasers are found in many everyday devices, too. They are used in the CD drive of computers and in many printers. Laser pointers can be used from a distance, and laser levelers can help you hang pictures in a straight line. Lasers are also used to make holograms, the three-dimensional images seen on credit cards.

Active Reading

12 Identify As you read, underline five specific uses of laser technology.

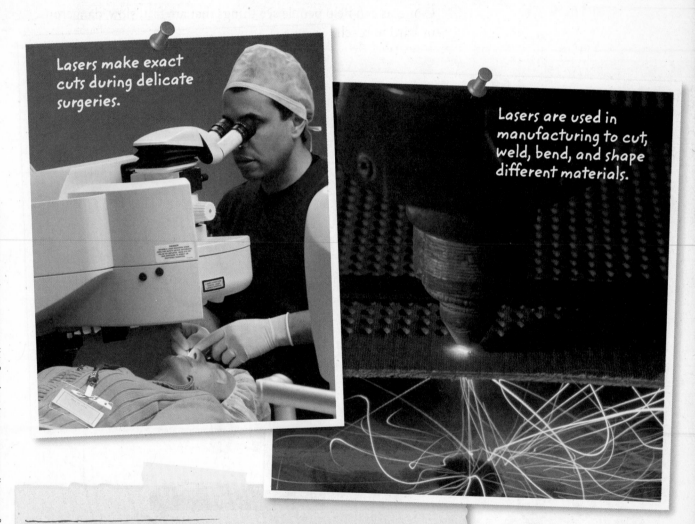

Lasers make exact cuts during delicate surgeries.

Lasers are used in manufacturing to cut, weld, bend, and shape different materials.

13 Infer The photographs on this page show medical and industrial applications of laser technology. Describe a household use of lasers.

_____

_____

_____

_____

Seeing is BELIEVING

What are some ways light can change what people see?

Optical instruments are devices that use mirrors and lenses to control the path of light and change what people can see. These light technologies help people see objects that cannot be observed with the eye alone. Microscopes allow people to see the very small; binoculars and telescopes can allow people to see the very far. Cameras can help people see things that are fast, slow, dangerous, or hard to reach.

Active Reading

14 Identify As you read, underline four examples of light technology that change what people see.

Microscopes

Microscopes are used to see magnified images of tiny, nearby objects. Simple light microscopes have two convex lenses. An objective lens is close to the object being studied. An eyepiece lens is the lens you look through. Light from a lamp or mirror at the bottom shines through the object being studied. The user looks through the eyepiece and focuses on the object.

Visualize It!

15 Identify Label the lenses in the illustration.

A

B

Green chloroplasts inside plant cells.

Microscopes allow us to see the very small objects in our world.

© Houghton Mifflin Harcourt Publishing Company • Image Credits: ©M. I. Walker/Photo Researchers, Inc.

Telescopes

Telescopes are used to see images of large, distant objects. Astronomers use telescopes to study known objects, like the moon, and to search for undiscovered objects. Telescopes that use visible light are classified as either refracting or reflecting. Refracting telescopes use lenses to collect light. Reflecting telescopes use mirrors to collect light. Large telescopes are often housed in observatories, high on mountaintops. The less atmosphere the light travels through, the clearer the image appears.

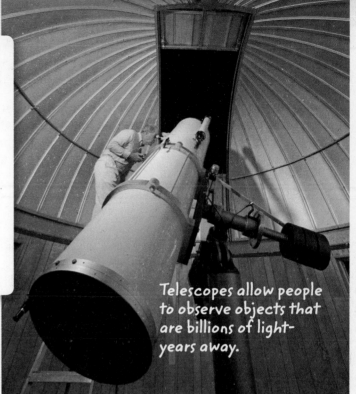

Telescopes allow people to observe objects that are billions of light-years away.

Cameras

Cameras are used to record images. A digital camera controls the light that enters the camera and uses sensors to detect the light. The sensors send an electrical signal to a computer in the camera. This signal contains data about the image that can be stored and transferred. Some cameras also record video using computers. Cameras are useful for scientists who need to see and record things that are fast, slow, dangerous, or hard to reach.

The lens of a digital camera focuses light on the sensors. Moving the lens focuses light from objects at different distances.

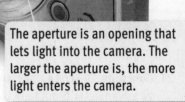

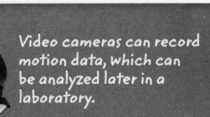

Video cameras can record motion data, which can be analyzed later in a laboratory.

The aperture is an opening that lets light into the camera. The larger the aperture is, the more light enters the camera.

Think Outside the Book

16 Summarize Choose one of the technologies on these two pages and research its history. Write a report of your findings.

Visual Summary

To complete this summary, fill in each blank with the correct word or phrase. Then use the key below to check your answers. You can use this page to review the main concepts of the lesson.

Light Technology

Light is produced in many different ways.

17 A(n) _____ bulb produces light more efficiently than a(n) _____ bulb does.

Light can be used to transfer information.

18 _____ can transmit telephone calls, network computers, and allow doctors to see inside the body.

Interactions between light and matter help humans perform tasks.

19 Lasers are useful in manufacturing because the light beam is narrow and carries a great amount of _____

Light can be manipulated to change what people can see.

20 A _____ telescope uses lenses to manipulate light and allow people to see far away objects.

Answers: 17 fluorescent, incandescent; 18 Optical fibers; 19 energy; 20 refracting

21 Conclude Describe three areas of human knowledge that would not be as advanced without light technology.

Lesson Review

Vocabulary

Fill in the blank with the term that best completes the following sentences.

1 The coating in a(n) _____ light bulb emits light when it interacts with ultraviolet light.

2 The material inside a(n) _____ light bulb emits light when it is very hot.

3 A(n) _____ contains solid materials that emit light when energized by an electric current.

4 Intense light of a narrow range of wavelengths

is called _____ light.

Key Concepts

5 List Give three examples of infrared technologies.

_____

_____

_____

6 Identify What light technology is used by GPS systems?

_____

7 Explain How can a camera help someone see something he or she wouldn't normally be able to see?

_____

_____

_____

_____

_____

_____

8 Distinguish In what way is laser light different from the light produced by other sources?

_____

_____

_____

_____

Critical Thinking

Use this drawing to answer the following questions.

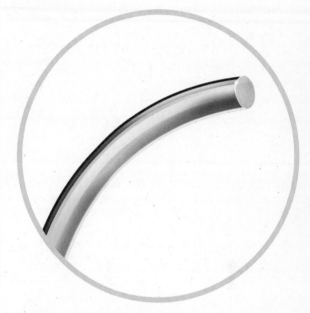

9 Illustrate Draw light rays on the fiber to show how light travels through, and is emitted from, an optical fiber.

10 Evaluate What are some advantages of optical fibers?

_____

_____

_____

_____

_____

11 Recommend Some streetlights use incandescent bulbs, and others use LEDs. Which would you recommend and why?

_____

_____

_____

_____

_____

My Notes

Lesson 1

ESSENTIAL QUESTION
What is the relationship between various EM waves?

Distinguish between the parts of the electromagnetic spectrum.

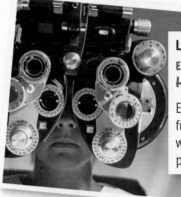

Lesson 4

ESSENTIAL QUESTION
How do people see?

Explain how the eye functions and works with the brain to produce vision.

Lesson 2

ESSENTIAL QUESTION
How does light interact with matter?

Explain how light and matter can interact.

Lesson 3

ESSENTIAL QUESTION
How do mirrors and lenses work?

Describe ways that lenses and mirrors form images.

Lesson 5

ESSENTIAL QUESTION
How can light be used?

Apply knowledge of light to describe light-related technologies.

Think Outside the Book

2 Synthesize Choose one of these activities to help synthesize what you have learned in this unit.

☐ Using what you learned in lessons 3 and 4, make a poster presentation explaining the ways in which lenses help people see better.

☐ Using what you learned in lessons 1, 2, and 5, and research, create a timeline showing how understanding the electromagnetic spectrum and the ways in which to apply it has affected communications technology.

Connect ESSENTIAL QUESTIONS
Lessons 1, 3, and 4

1 Synthesize What type of light forms a reflected image in a mirror? Would you expect that a mirror would reflect ultraviolet light? Explain.

_____

_____

_____

_____

Name _____

Vocabulary

Check the box to show whether each statement is true or false.

T	F	
☐	☐	**1** A <u>convex</u> mirror curves outward like the back of a spoon.
☐	☐	**2** <u>Laser</u> light is more intense than other types of light because it comes from a very small range of wavelengths in the visible spectrum.
☐	☐	**3** Electromagnetic waves travel through a medium by <u>radiation</u>.
☐	☐	**4** <u>Scattering</u> occurs when certain wavelengths of light are reflected by particles, causing the light to spread out in all directions
☐	☐	**5** A material that allows light to pass through it completely is <u>transparent</u>.

Key Concepts

Read each question below, and circle the best answer.

6 Which statement best explains why most people can see colors?

A The eyes and brain can see all wavelengths in the electromagnetic spectrum.

B The eyes and brain rely on all of the radiation from the sun to see colors.

C The eyes and brain interpret different wavelengths of visible light as different colors.

D The eyes and brain see light waves only when they travel through a medium.

7 What type of cells in the retina are involved in detecting light?

A the lens and the cornea

B rod cells and lenses

C rod cells and cone cells

D cone cells and corneas

8 The table below lists electromagnetic waves.

	A	B	C	D
Low frequency	Radio waves	Gamma rays	Laser light	Visible light
	Microwaves	x-rays	Visible light	x-rays
	Infrared waves	Ultraviolet light	Ultraviolet light	Ultraviolet light
	Visible light	Visible light	x-rays	Radio waves
High frequency	Ultraviolet light	Infrared light	Gamma rays	Microwaves

Which column correctly lists waves from lowest to highest frequencies?

A Column A

B Column B

C Column C

D Column D

9 Which statement best tells the ways in which light interacts with matter?

A Light can come from the sun, fire, or a light bulb.

B Light waves can be reflected, refracted, or absorbed by matter.

C Laser light goes through matter, and all other light gets stopped by matter.

D Only visible light can interact with matter.

10 Waves of red light and yellow light go through air and strike a piece of glass. The diagram shows how the two kinds of light interact with the glass.

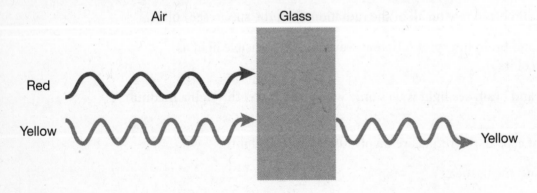

Which statement describes how the glass interacts with red and yellow light?

A The glass absorbs red light and transmits yellow light.

B The glass transmits red light and absorbs yellow light.

C The glass reflects both red and yellow light.

D The glass transmits both red and yellow light.

11 A beam of incoming light strikes a flat mirror. The mirror reflects the light.

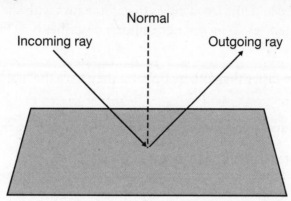

Which statement best explains what this diagram of a light ray and a mirror is showing?

A A mirror scatters most of the light that strikes its surface.

B The normal absorbs rays of light that strike the surface of a mirror.

C The normal measures the angle of a light ray reflecting off the surface of a flat mirror.

D The angle of an incoming ray is used to predict the angle of the normal when light strikes the surface.

12 When Juan shined a light through the liquid in glass A and then glass B, he saw that the liquids in the two glasses looked different.

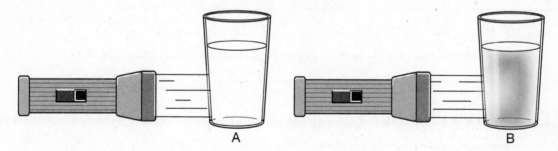

What did the liquids' appearance tell about how light was interacting with them?

A The liquid in glass A absorbed light; the liquid in glass B reflected light.

B The liquid in glass A was transparent; the liquid in glass B was translucent.

C The liquid in glass A was translucent; the liquid in glass B was transparent.

D The liquids looked different because the liquid in glass A scattered more light than the liquid in glass B.

13 The electromagnetic spectrum includes all electromagnetic waves, from radio waves with long wavelengths and low frequencies to gamma rays with short wavelengths and high frequencies. Which statement best describes how fast these waves travel in a vacuum?

A Gamma rays travel much faster than others because they have the highest frequencies.

B High frequency waves travel somewhat faster than low frequency waves

C Infrared waves travel faster than ultraviolet waves.

D All electromagnetic waves travel at the same speed.

Critical Thinking

Answer the following questions in the space provided.

14 Explain what the cornea is and how it interacts with light. What is the role of the retina in vision?

_____

_____

15 Name three main shapes that mirrors can have. What is the difference between converging and diverging mirrors? Describe real and virtual images.

_____

_____

_____

_____

_____

Connect **ESSENTIAL QUESTIONS**
Lessons 1, 4, and 5

Answer the following question in the space provided.

16 Give two examples of natural light and two examples of artificial light. How is natural light transmitted? How is artificial light produced?

_____

_____

_____

_____

Look It Up!

© Houghton Mifflin Harcourt Publishing Company

References

Mineral Properties

Here are five steps to take in mineral identification:

1 Determine the color of the mineral. Is it light-colored, dark-colored, or a specific color?

2 Determine the luster of the mineral. Is it metallic or non-metallic?

3 Determine the color of any powder left by its streak.

4 Determine the hardness of your mineral. Is it soft, hard, or very hard? Using a glass plate, see if the mineral scratches it.

5 Determine whether your sample has cleavage or any special properties.

TERMS TO KNOW	DEFINITION
adamantine	a non-metallic luster like that of a diamond
cleavage	how a mineral breaks when subject to stress on a particular plane
luster	the state or quality of shining by reflecting light
streak	the color of a mineral when it is powdered
submetallic	between metallic and nonmetallic in luster
vitreous	glass-like type of luster

Silicate Minerals

Mineral	Color	Luster	Streak	Hardness	Cleavage and Special Properties
Beryl	deep green, pink, white, bluish green, or yellow	vitreous	white	7.5–8	1 cleavage direction; some varieties fluoresce in ultraviolet light
Chlorite	green	vitreous to pearly	pale green	2–2.5	1 cleavage direction
Garnet	green, red, brown, black	vitreous	white	6.5–7.5	no cleavage
Hornblende	dark green, brown, or black	vitreous	none	5–6	2 cleavage directions
Muscovite	colorless, silvery white, or brown	vitreous or pearly	white	2–2.5	1 cleavage direction
Olivine	olive green, yellow	vitreous	white or none	6.5–7	no cleavage
Orthoclase	colorless, white, pink, or other colors	vitreous	white or none	6	2 cleavage directions
Plagioclase	colorless, white, yellow, pink, green	vitreous	white	6	2 cleavage directions
Quartz	colorless or white; any color when not pure	vitreous or waxy	white or none	7	no cleavage

Nonsilicate Minerals					
Mineral	**Color**	**Luster**	**Streak**	**Hardness**	**Cleavage and Special Properties**
Native Elements					
Copper	copper-red	metallic	copper-red	2.5–3	no cleavage
Diamond	pale yellow or colorless	adamantine	none	10	4 cleavage directions
Graphite	black to gray	submetallic	black	1–2	1 cleavage direction
Carbonates					
Aragonite	colorless, white, or pale yellow	vitreous	white	3.5–4	2 cleavage directions; reacts with hydrochloric acid
Calcite	colorless or white to tan	vitreous	white	3	3 cleavage directions; reacts with weak acid; double refraction
Halides					
Fluorite	light green, yellow, purple, bluish green, or other colors	vitreous	none	4	4 cleavage directions; some varieties fluoresce
Halite	white	vitreous	white	2.0–2.5	3 cleavage directions
Oxides					
Hematite	reddish brown to black	metallic to earthy	dark red to red-brown	5.6–6.5	no cleavage; magnetic when heated
Magnetite	iron-black	metallic	black	5.5–6.5	no cleavage; magnetic
Sulfates					
Anhydrite	colorless, bluish, or violet	vitreous to pearly	white	3–3.5	3 cleavage directions
Gypsum	white, pink, gray, or colorless	vitreous, pearly, or silky	white	2.0	3 cleavage directions
Sulfides					
Galena	lead-gray	metallic	lead-gray to black	2.5–2.8	3 cleavage directions
Pyrite	brassy yellow	metallic	greenish, brownish, or black	6–6.5	no cleavage

References

Geologic Time Scale

Geologists developed the geologic time scale to represent the 4.6 billion years of Earth's history that have passed since Earth formed. This scale divides Earth's history into blocks of time. The boundaries between these time intervals (shown in millions of years ago or mya in the table below), represent major changes in Earth's history. Some boundaries are defined by mass extinctions, major changes in Earth's surface, and/or major changes in Earth's climate.

The four major divisions that encompass the history of life on Earth are Precambrian time, the Paleozoic era, the Mesozoic era, and the Cenozoic era. The largest divisions are eons. **Precambrian time** is made up of the first three eons, over 4 billion years of Earth's history.

The **Paleozoic era** lasted from 542 mya to 251 mya. All major plant groups, except flowering plants, appeared during this era. By the end of the era, reptiles, winged insects, and fishes had also appeared. The largest known mass extinction occurred at the end of this era.

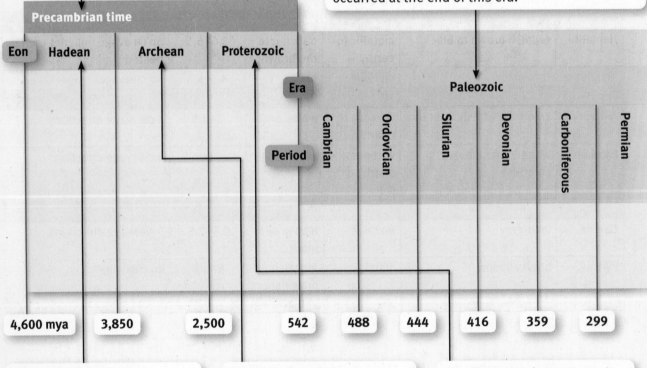

Precambrian time				Paleozoic					
Eon Hadean	Archean	Proterozoic	**Era**						
			Period Cambrian	Ordovician	Silurian	Devonian	Carboniferous	Permian	
4,600 mya	3,850	2,500	542	488	444	416	359	299	

The **Hadean eon** lasted from about 4.6 billion years ago (bya) to 3.85 bya. It is described based on evidence from meterorites and rocks from the moon.

The **Archean eon** lasted from 3.85 bya to 2.5 bya. The earliest rocks from Earth that have been found and dated formed at the start of this eon.

The **Proterozoic eon** lasted from 2.5 bya to 542 mya. The first organisms, which were single-celled organisms, appeared during this eon. These organisms produced so much oxygen that they changed Earth's oceans and Earth's atmosphere.

Divisions of Time

The divisions of time shown here represent major changes in Earth's surface and when life developed and changed significantly on Earth. As new evidence is found, the boundaries of these divisions may shift. The Phanerozoic eon is divided into three eras. The beginning of each of these eras represents a change in the types of organisms that dominated Earth. And, each era is commonly characterized by the types of organisms that dominated the era. These eras are divided into periods, and periods are divided into epochs.

The **Mesozoic era** lasted from 251 mya to 65.5 mya. During this era, many kinds of dinosaurs dominated land, and giant lizards swam in the ocean. The first birds, mammals, and flowering plants also appeared during this time. About two-thirds of all land species went extinct at the end of this era.

The **Phanerozoic eon** began 542 mya. We live in this eon.

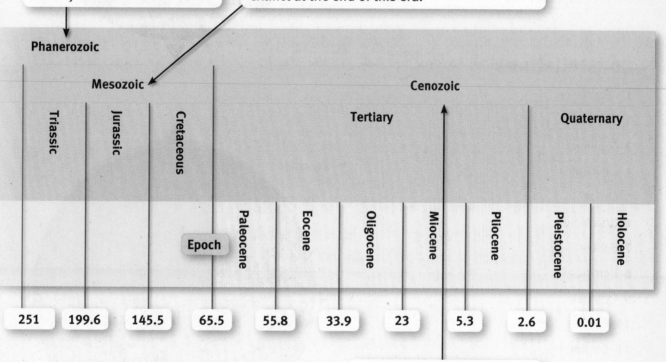

Phanerozoic

Mesozoic

Cenozoic

| Triassic | Jurassic | Cretaceous | | Tertiary | | | | Quaternary | |

Epoch — Paleocene, Eocene, Oligocene, Miocene, Pliocene, Pleistocene, Holocene

| 251 | 199.6 | 145.5 | 65.5 | 55.8 | 33.9 | 23 | 5.3 | 2.6 | 0.01 |

The **Cenozoic era** began 65.5 mya and continues today. Mammals dominate this era. During the Mesozoic era, mammals were small in size but grew much larger during the Cenozoic era. Primates, including humans, appeared during this era.

References

Star Charts for the Northern Hemisphere

A star chart is a map of the stars in the night sky. It shows the names and positions of constellations and major stars. Star charts can be used to identify constellations and even to orient yourself using Polaris, the North Star.

Because Earth moves through space, different constellations are visible at different times of the year. The star charts on these pages show the constellations visible during each season in the Northern Hemisphere.

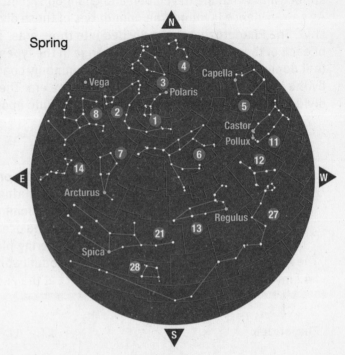

Spring

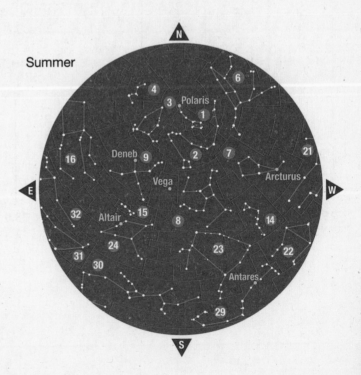

Summer

Constellations

1 Ursa Minor

2 Draco

3 Cepheus

4 Cassiopeia

5 Auriga

6 Ursa Major

7 Boötes

8 Hercules

9 Cygnus

10 Perseus

11 Gemini

12 Cancer

13 Leo

14 Serpens

15 Sagitta

16 Pegasus

17 Pisces

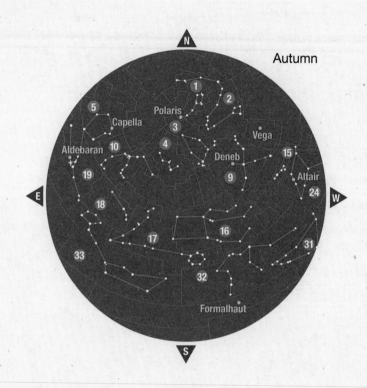

Autumn

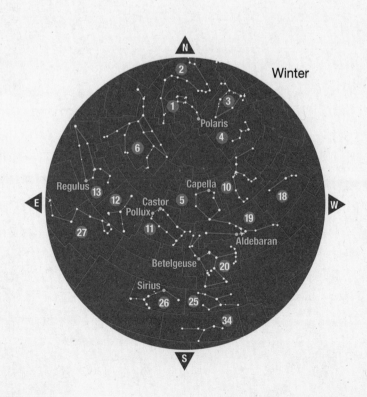

Winter

Constellations

18 Aries

19 Taurus

20 Orion

21 Virgo

22 Libra

23 Ophiuchus

24 Aquila

25 Lepus

26 Canis Major

27 Hydra

28 Corvus

29 Scorpius

30 Sagittarius

31 Capricornus

32 Aquarius

33 Cetus

34 Columba

World Map

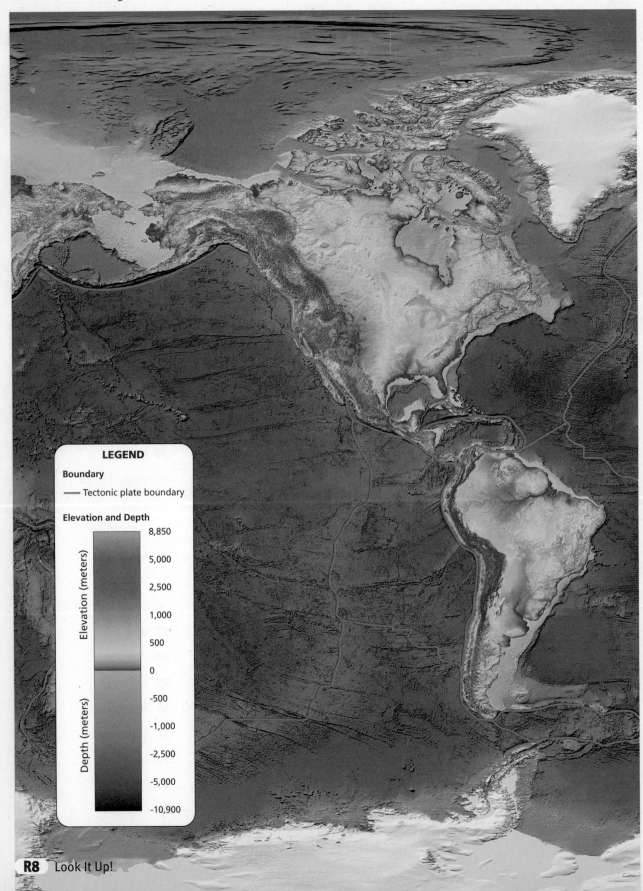

LEGEND

Boundary

— Tectonic plate boundary

Elevation and Depth

Elevation (meters)

8,850
5,000
2,500
1,000
500
0

Depth (meters)

-500
-1,000
-2,500
-5,000
-10,900

References

Classification of Living Things

Domains and Kingdoms

All organisms belong to one of three domains: Domain Archaea, Domain Bacteria, or Domain Eukarya. Some of the groups within these domains are shown below. (Remember that genus names are italicized.)

Domain Archaea

The organisms in this domain are single-celled prokaryotes, many of which live in extreme environments.

Archaea		
Group	**Example**	**Characteristics**
Methanogens	*Methanococcus*	produce methane gas; can't live in oxygen
Thermophiles	*Sulpholobus*	require sulphur; can't live in oxygen
Halophiles	*Halococcus*	live in very salty environments; most can live in oxygen

Domain Bacteria

Organisms in this domain are single-celled prokaryotes and are found in almost every environment on Earth.

Bacteria		
Group	**Example**	**Characteristics**
Bacilli	*Escherichia*	rod shaped; some bacilli fix nitrogen; some cause disease
Cocci	*Streptococcus*	spherical shaped; some cause disease; can form spores
Spirilla	*Treponema*	spiral shaped; cause diseases such as syphilis and Lyme disease

Domain Eukarya

Organisms in this domain are single-celled or multicellular eukaryotes.

Kingdom Protista Many protists resemble fungi, plants, or animals, but are smaller and simpler in structure. Most are single celled.

Protists		
Group	**Example**	**Characteristics**
Sarcodines	*Amoeba*	radiolarians; single-celled consumers
Ciliates	*Paramecium*	single-celled consumers
Flagellates	*Trypanosoma*	single-celled parasites
Sporozoans	*Plasmodium*	single-celled parasites
Euglenas	*Euglena*	single celled; photosynthesize
Diatoms	*Pinnularia*	most are single celled; photosynthesize
Dinoflagellates	*Gymnodinium*	single celled; some photosynthesize
Algae	*Volvox*	single celled or multicellular; photosynthesize
Slime molds	*Physarum*	single celled or multicellular; consumers or decomposers
Water molds	powdery mildew	single celled or multicellular; parasites or decomposers

Kingdom Fungi Most fungi are multicellular. Their cells have thick cell walls. Fungi absorb food from their environment.

Fungi		
Group	**Examples**	**Characteristics**
Threadlike fungi	bread mold	spherical; decomposers
Sac fungi	yeast; morels	saclike; parasites and decomposers
Club fungi	mushrooms; rusts; smuts	club shaped; parasites and decomposers
Lichens	British soldier	a partnership between a fungus and an alga

Kingdom Plantae Plants are multicellular and have cell walls made of cellulose. Plants make their own food through photosynthesis. Plants are classified into divisions instead of phyla.

Plants		
Group	**Examples**	**Characteristics**
Bryophytes	mosses; liverworts	no vascular tissue; reproduce by spores
Club mosses	*Lycopodium;* ground pine	grow in wooded areas; reproduce by spores
Horsetails	rushes	grow in wetland areas; reproduce by spores
Ferns	spleenworts; sensitive fern	large leaves called fronds; reproduce by spores
Conifers	pines; spruces; firs	needlelike leaves; reproduce by seeds made in cones
Cycads	*Zamia*	slow growing; reproduce by seeds made in large cones
Gnetophytes	*Welwitschia*	only three living families; reproduce by seeds
Ginkgoes	*Ginkgo*	only one living species; reproduce by seeds
Angiosperms	all flowering plants	reproduce by seeds made in flowers; fruit

Kingdom Animalia Animals are multicellular. Their cells do not have cell walls. Most animals have specialized tissues and complex organ systems. Animals get food by eating other organisms.

Animals		
Group	**Examples**	**Characteristics**
Sponges	glass sponges	no symmetry or specialized tissues; aquatic
Cnidarians	jellyfish; coral	radial symmetry; aquatic
Flatworms	planaria; tapeworms; flukes	bilateral symmetry; organ systems
Roundworms	*Trichina;* hookworms	bilateral symmetry; organ systems
Annelids	earthworms; leeches	bilateral symmetry; organ systems
Mollusks	snails; octopuses	bilateral symmetry; organ systems
Echinoderms	sea stars; sand dollars	radial symmetry; organ systems
Arthropods	insects; spiders; lobsters	bilateral symmetry; organ systems
Chordates	fish; amphibians; reptiles; birds; mammals	bilateral symmetry; complex organ systems

References

Periodic Table of the Elements

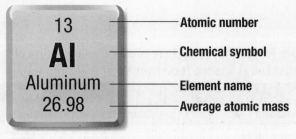

- 13 — Atomic number
- Al — Chemical symbol
- Aluminum — Element name
- 26.98 — Average atomic mass

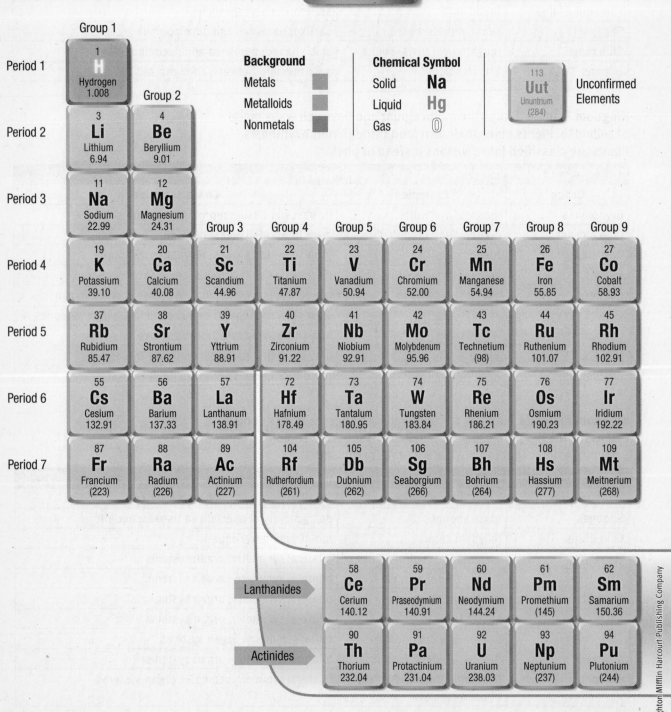

Background
- Metals
- Metalloids
- Nonmetals

Chemical Symbol
- Solid — Na
- Liquid — Hg
- Gas — O

113 Uut Ununtrium (284) — Unconfirmed Elements

Group 1								
Period 1 — 1 H Hydrogen 1.008								

Group 1	Group 2

| Period 2 — 3 Li Lithium 6.94 | 4 Be Beryllium 9.01 |

| Period 3 — 11 Na Sodium 22.99 | 12 Mg Magnesium 24.31 |

Group 3	Group 4	Group 5	Group 6	Group 7	Group 8	Group 9
Period 4 — 19 K Potassium 39.10	20 Ca Calcium 40.08	21 Sc Scandium 44.96	22 Ti Titanium 47.87	23 V Vanadium 50.94	24 Cr Chromium 52.00	25 Mn Manganese 54.94	26 Fe Iron 55.85	27 Co Cobalt 58.93
Period 5 — 37 Rb Rubidium 85.47	38 Sr Strontium 87.62	39 Y Yttrium 88.91	40 Zr Zirconium 91.22	41 Nb Niobium 92.91	42 Mo Molybdenum 95.96	43 Tc Technetium (98)	44 Ru Ruthenium 101.07	45 Rh Rhodium 102.91
Period 6 — 55 Cs Cesium 132.91	56 Ba Barium 137.33	57 La Lanthanum 138.91	72 Hf Hafnium 178.49	73 Ta Tantalum 180.95	74 W Tungsten 183.84	75 Re Rhenium 186.21	76 Os Osmium 190.23	77 Ir Iridium 192.22
Period 7 — 87 Fr Francium (223)	88 Ra Radium (226)	89 Ac Actinium (227)	104 Rf Rutherfordium (261)	105 Db Dubnium (262)	106 Sg Seaborgium (266)	107 Bh Bohrium (264)	108 Hs Hassium (277)	109 Mt Meitnerium (268)

Lanthanides

58 Ce Cerium 140.12	59 Pr Praseodymium 140.91	60 Nd Neodymium 144.24	61 Pm Promethium (145)	62 Sm Samarium 150.36

Actinides

90 Th Thorium 232.04	91 Pa Protactinium 231.04	92 U Uranium 238.03	93 Np Neptunium (237)	94 Pu Plutonium (244)

The International Union of Pure and Applied Chemistry (IUPAC) has determined that, because of isotopic variance, the average atomic mass is best represented by a range of values for each of the following elements: hydrogen, lithium, boron, carbon, nitrogen, oxygen, silicon, sulfur, chlorine, and thallium. However, the values in this table are appropriate for everyday calculations.

			Group 13	Group 14	Group 15	Group 16	Group 17	Group 18
								2 **He** Helium 4.003
			5 **B** Boron 10.81	6 **C** Carbon 12.01	7 **N** Nitrogen 14.01	8 **O** Oxygen 16.00	9 **F** Fluorine 19.00	10 **Ne** Neon 20.18
Group 10	Group 11	Group 12	13 **Al** Aluminum 26.98	14 **Si** Silicon 28.09	15 **P** Phosphorus 30.97	16 **S** Sulfur 32.06	17 **Cl** Chlorine 35.45	18 **Ar** Argon 39.95
28 **Ni** Nickel 58.69	29 **Cu** Copper 63.55	30 **Zn** Zinc 65.38	31 **Ga** Gallium 69.72	32 **Ge** Germanium 72.63	33 **As** Arsenic 74.92	34 **Se** Selenium 78.96	35 **Br** Bromine 79.90	36 **Kr** Krypton 83.80
46 **Pd** Palladium 106.42	47 **Ag** Silver 107.87	48 **Cd** Cadmium 112.41	49 **In** Indium 114.82	50 **Sn** Tin 118.71	51 **Sb** Antimony 121.76	52 **Te** Tellurium 127.60	53 **I** Iodine 126.90	54 **Xe** Xenon 131.29
78 **Pt** Platinum 195.08	79 **Au** Gold 196.97	80 **Hg** Mercury 200.59	81 **Tl** Thallium 204.38	82 **Pb** Lead 207.2	83 **Bi** Bismuth 208.98	84 **Po** Polonium (209)	85 **At** Astatine (210)	86 **Rn** Radon (222)
110 **Ds** Darmstadtium (271)	111 **Rg** Roentgenium (272)	112 **Cn** Copernicium (285)	113 **Uut** Ununtrium (284)	114 **Uuq** Ununquadium (289)	115 **Uup** Ununpentium (288)	116 **Uuh** Ununhexium (292)	117 **Uus** Ununseptium (294)	118 **Uuo** Ununoctium (294)

63 **Eu** Europium 151.96	64 **Gd** Gadolinium 157.25	65 **Tb** Terbium 158.93	66 **Dy** Dysprosium 162.50	67 **Ho** Holmium 164.93	68 **Er** Erbium 167.26	69 **Tm** Thulium 168.93	70 **Yb** Ytterbium 173.05	71 **Lu** Lutetium 174.97
95 **Am** Americium (243)	96 **Cm** Curium (247)	97 **Bk** Berkelium (247)	98 **Cf** Californium (251)	99 **Es** Einsteinium (252)	100 **Fm** Fermium (257)	101 **Md** Mendelevium (258)	102 **No** Nobelium (259)	103 **Lr** Lawrencium (262)

© Houghton Mifflin Harcourt Publishing Company

References

Physical Science Refresher

Atoms and Elements

Every object in the universe is made of matter. **Matter** is anything that takes up space and has mass. All matter is made of atoms. An **atom** is the smallest particle into which an element can be divided and still be the same element. An **element**, in turn, is a substance that cannot be broken down into simpler substances by chemical means. Each element consists of only one kind of atom. An element may be made of many atoms, but they are all the same kind of atom.

Atomic Structure

Atoms are made of smaller particles called **electrons**, **protons**, and **neutrons**. Electrons have a negative electric charge, protons have a positive charge, and neutrons have no electric charge. Together, protons and neutrons form the **nucleus**, or small dense center, of an atom. Because protons are positively charged and neutrons are neutral, the nucleus has a positive charge. Electrons move within an area around the nucleus called the **electron cloud**. Electrons move so quickly that scientists cannot determine their exact speeds and positions at the same time.

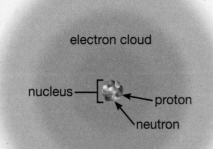

electron cloud

nucleus — proton

neutron

Atomic Number

To help distinguish one element from another, scientists use the atomic numbers of atoms. The **atomic number** is the number of protons in the nucleus of an atom. The atoms of a certain element always have the same number of protons.

When atoms have an equal number of protons and electrons, they are uncharged, or electrically neutral. The atomic number equals the number of electrons in an uncharged atom. The number of neutrons, however, can vary for a given element. Atoms of the same element that have different numbers of neutrons are called **isotopes**.

Periodic Table of the Elements

In the periodic table, each element in the table is in a separate box. And the elements are arranged from left to right in order of increasing atomic number. That is, an uncharged atom of each element has one more electron and one more proton than an uncharged atom of the element to its left. Each horizontal row of the table is called a **period**. Changes in chemical properties of elements across a period correspond to changes in the electron arrangements of their atoms.

Each vertical column of the table is known as a **group**. A group lists elements with similar physical and chemical properties. For this reason, a group is also sometimes called a family. The elements in a group have similar properties because their atoms have the same number of electrons in their outer energy level. For example, the elements helium, neon, argon, krypton, xenon, and radon all have similar properties and are known as the noble gases.

Molecules and Compounds

When two or more elements join chemically, they form a **compound**. A compound is a new substance with properties different from those of the elements that compose it. For example, water, H_2O, is a compound formed when hydrogen (H) and oxygen (O) combine. The smallest complete unit of a compound that has the properties of that compound is called a **molecule**. A chemical formula indicates the elements in a compound. It also indicates the relative number of atoms of each element in the compound. The chemical formula for water is H_2O. So, each water molecule consists of two atoms of hydrogen and one atom of oxygen. The subscript number after the symbol for an element shows how many atoms of that element are in a single molecule of the compound.

Chemical Equations

A chemical reaction occurs when a chemical change takes place. A chemical equation describes a chemical reaction using chemical formulas. The equation indicates the substances that react and the substances that are produced. For example, when carbon and oxygen combine, they can form carbon dioxide, shown in the equation below: $C + O_2 \longrightarrow CO_2$

Acids, Bases, and pH

An **ion** is an atom or group of chemically bonded atoms that has an electric charge because it has lost or gained one or more electrons. When an acid, such as hydrochloric acid, HCl, is mixed with water, it separates into ions. An **acid** is a compound that produces hydrogen ions, H^+, in water. The hydrogen ions then combine with a water molecule to form a hydronium ion, H_3O^+. A **base**, on the other hand, is a substance that produces hydroxide ions, OH^-, in water.

To determine whether a solution is acidic or basic, scientists use pH. The **pH** of a solution is a measure of the hydronium ion concentration in a solution. The pH scale ranges from 0 to 14. Acids have a pH that is less than 7. The lower the number, the more acidic the solution. The middle point, pH = 7, is neutral, neither acidic nor basic. Bases have a pH that is greater than 7. The higher the number is, the more basic the solution.

The pH of Some Common Materials

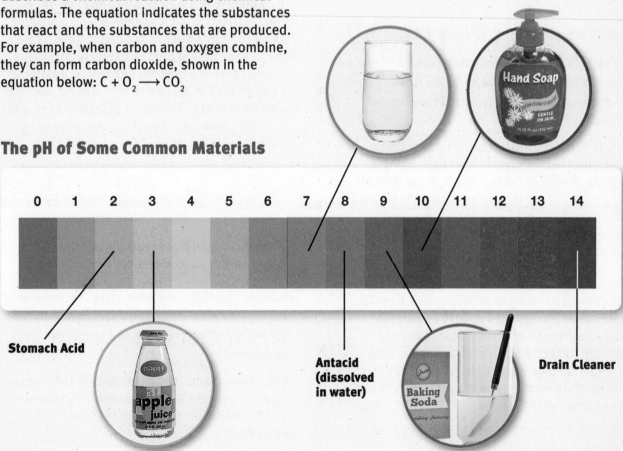

Stomach Acid

Antacid (dissolved in water)

Baking Soda

Drain Cleaner

Hand Soap

References

Physical Laws and Useful Equations

Law of Conservation of Mass

Mass cannot be created or destroyed during ordinary chemical or physical changes.

The total mass in a closed system is always the same no matter how many physical changes or chemical reactions occur.

Law of Conservation of Energy

Energy can be neither created nor destroyed.

The total amount of energy in a closed system is always the same. Energy can be changed from one form to another, but all of the different forms of energy in a system always add up to the same total amount of energy, no matter how many energy conversions occur.

Law of Universal Gravitation

All objects in the universe attract each other by a force called gravity. The size of the force depends on the masses of the objects and the distance between the objects.

The first part of the law explains why lifting a bowling ball is much harder than lifting a marble. Because the bowling ball has a much larger mass than the marble does, the amount of gravity between Earth and the bowling ball is greater than the amount of gravity between Earth and the marble.

The second part of the law explains why a satellite can remain in orbit around Earth. The satellite is placed at a carefully calculated distance from Earth. This distance is great enough to keep Earth's gravity from pulling the satellite down, yet small enough to keep the satellite from escaping Earth's gravity and wandering off into space.

Newton's Laws of Motion

Newton's first law of motion states that an object at rest remains at rest, and an object in motion remains in motion at constant speed and in a straight line unless acted on by an unbalanced force.

The first part of the law explains why a football will remain on a tee until it is kicked off or until a gust of wind blows it off. The second part of the law explains why a bike rider will continue moving forward after the bike comes to an abrupt stop. Gravity and the friction of the sidewalk will eventually stop the rider.

Newton's second law of motion states that the acceleration of an object depends on the mass of the object and the amount of force applied.

The first part of the law explains why the acceleration of a 4 kg bowling ball will be greater than the acceleration of a 6 kg bowling ball if the same force is applied to both balls. The second part of the law explains why the acceleration of a bowling ball will be greater if a larger force is applied to the bowling ball. The relationship of acceleration (a) to mass (m) and force (F) can be expressed mathematically by the following equation:

$$acceleration = \frac{force}{mass}, \text{ or } a = \frac{F}{m}$$

This equation is often rearranged to read *force = mass* $\times$ acceleration, or $F = m \times a$

Newton's third law of motion states that whenever one object exerts a force on a second object, the second object exerts an equal and opposite force on the first.

This law explains that a runner is able to move forward because the ground exerts an equal and opposite force on the runner's foot after each step.

Average speed

$$\text{average speed} = \frac{\text{total distance}}{\text{total time}}$$

Example:
A bicycle messenger traveled a distance of 136 km in 8 h. What was the messenger's average speed?

$$\frac{136 \text{ km}}{8 \text{ h}} = 17 \text{ km/h}$$

The messenger's average speed was **17 km/h**.

Average acceleration

$$\text{average acceleration} = \frac{\text{final velocity} - \text{starting velocity}}{\text{time it takes to change velocity}}$$

Example:
Calculate the average acceleration of an Olympic 100 m dash sprinter who reached a velocity of 20 m/s south at the finish line. The race was in a straight line and lasted 10 s.

$$\frac{20 \text{ m/s} - 0 \text{ m/s}}{10 \text{ s}} = 2 \text{ m/s/s}$$

The sprinter's average acceleration was **2 m/s/s south**.

Net force
Forces in the Same Direction

When forces are in the same direction, add the forces together to determine the net force.

Example:
Calculate the net force on a stalled car that is being pushed by two people. One person is pushing with a force of 13 N northwest, and the other person is pushing with a force of 8 N in the same direction.

$$13 \text{ N} + 8 \text{ N} = 21 \text{ N}$$

The net force is **21 N northwest**.

Forces in Opposite Directions

When forces are in opposite directions, subtract the smaller force from the larger force to determine the net force. The net force will be in the direction of the larger force.

Example:
Calculate the net force on a rope that is being pulled on each end. One person is pulling on one end of the rope with a force of 12 N south. Another person is pulling on the opposite end of the rope with a force of 7 N north.

$$12 \text{ N} - 7 \text{ N} = 5 \text{ N}$$

The net force is **5 N south**.

Pressure

Pressure is the force exerted over a given area. The SI unit for pressure is the pascal. Its symbol is Pa.

$$\text{pressure} = \frac{\text{force}}{\text{area}}$$

Example:
Calculate the pressure of the air in a soccer ball if the air exerts a force of 10 N over an area of 0.5 m^2.

$$\text{pressure} = \frac{10 N}{0.5 \text{ m}^2} = \frac{20 N}{m^2} = 20 \text{ Pa}$$

The pressure of the air inside the soccer ball is **20 Pa**.

Reading and Study Skills

A How-To Manual for Active Reading

This book belongs to you, and you are invited to write in it. In fact, the book won't be complete until you do. Sometimes you'll answer a question or follow directions to mark up the text. Other times you'll write down your own thoughts. And when you're done reading and writing in the book, the book will be ready to help you review what you learned and prepare for tests.

Active Reading Annotations

Before you read, you'll often come upon an Active Reading prompt that asks you to underline certain words or number the steps in a process. Here's an example.

Active Reading

12 Identify In this paragraph, number the sequence of sentences that describe replication.

Marking the text this way is called **annotating,** and your marks are called **annotations.** Annotating the text can help you identify important concepts while you read.

There are other ways that you can annotate the text. You can draw an asterisk (*) by vocabulary terms, mark unfamiliar or confusing terms and information with a question mark (?), and mark main ideas with a <u>double underline</u>. And you can even invent your own marks to annotate the text!

Other Annotating Opportunities

Keep your pencil, pen, or highlighter nearby as you read, so you can make a note or highlight an important point at any time. Here are a few ideas to get you started.

- Notice the headings in red and blue. The blue headings are questions that point to the main idea of what you're reading. The red headings are answers to the questions in the blue ones. Together these headings outline the content of the lesson. After reading a lesson, you could write your own answers to the questions.

- Notice the bold-faced words that are highlighted in yellow. They are highlighted so that you can easily find them again on the page where they are defined. As you read or as you review, challenge yourself to write your own sentence using the bold-faced term.

- Make a note in the margin at any time. You might
  - Ask a "What if" question
  - Comment on what you read
  - Make a connection to something you read elsewhere
  - Make a logical conclusion from the text

Use your own language and abbreviations. Invent a code, such as using circles and boxes around words to remind you of their importance or relation to each other. Your annotations will help you remember your questions for class discussions, and when you go back to the lesson later, you may be able to fill in what you didn't understand the first time you read it. Like a scientist in the field or in a lab, you will be recording your questions and observations for analysis later.

Active Reading Questions

After you read, you'll often come upon Active Reading questions that ask you to think about what you've just read. You'll write your answer underneath the question. Here's an example.

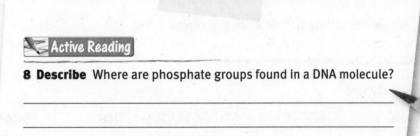

Active Reading

8 Describe Where are phosphate groups found in a DNA molecule?

This type of question helps you sum up what you've just read and pull out the most important ideas from the passage. In this case the question asks you to **describe** the structure of a DNA molecule that you have just read about. Other times you may be asked to do such things as **apply** a concept, **compare** two concepts, **summarize** a process, or **identify a cause-and-effect** relationship. You'll be strengthening those critical thinking skills that you'll use often in learning about science.

Reading and Study Skills

Using Graphic Organizers to Take Notes

Graphic organizers help you remember information as you read it for the first time and as you study it later. There are dozens of graphic organizers to choose from, so the first trick is to choose the one that's best suited to your purpose. Following are some graphic organizers to use for different purposes.

To remember lots of information	To relate a central idea to subordinate details	To describe a process	To make a comparison
• Arrange data in a Content Frame • Use Combination Notes to describe a concept in words and pictures	• Show relationships with a Mind Map or a Main Idea Web • Sum up relationships among many things with a Concept Map	• Use a Process Diagram to explain a procedure • Show a chain of events and results in a Cause-and-Effect Chart	• Compare two or more closely related things in a Venn Diagram

Content Frame

1 Make a four-column chart.

2 Fill the first column with categories (e.g., snail, ant, earthworm) and the first row with descriptive information (e.g., group, characteristic, appearance).

3 Fill the chart with details that belong in each row and column.

4 When you finish, you'll have a study aid that helps you compare one category to another.

Invertebrates

NAME	GROUP	CHARACTERISTICS	DRAWING
snail	mollusks	mangle	
ant	arthropods	six legs, exoskeleton	
earthworm	segmented worms	segmented body, circulatory and digestive systems	
heartworm	roundworms	digestive system	
sea star	echinoderms	spiny skin, tube feet	
jellyfish	cnidarians	stinging cells	

Combination Notes

1 Make a two-column chart.

2 Write descriptive words and definitions in the first column.

3 Draw a simple sketch that helps you remember the meaning of the term in the second column.

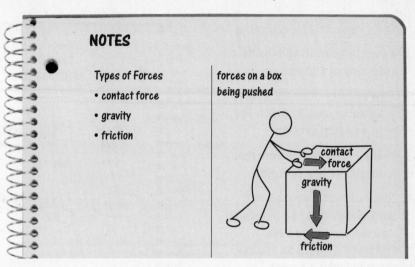

Mind Map

1 Draw an oval, and inside it write a topic to analyze.

2 Draw two or more arms extending from the oval. Each arm represents a main idea about the topic.

3 Draw lines from the arms on which to write details about each of the main ideas.

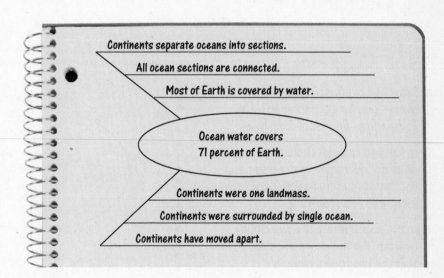

Main Idea Web

1 Make a box and write a concept you want to remember inside it.

2 Draw boxes around the central box, and label each one with a category of information about the concept (e.g., definition, formula, descriptive details).

3 Fill in the boxes with relevant details as you read.

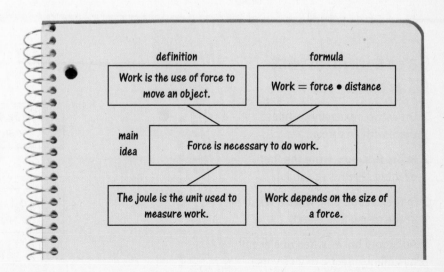

Reading and Study Skills

Concept Map

1 Draw a large oval, and inside it write a major concept.

2 Draw an arrow from the concept to a smaller oval, in which you write a related concept.

3 On the arrow, write a verb that connects the two concepts.

4 Continue in this way, adding ovals and arrows in a branching structure, until you have explained as much as you can about the main concept.

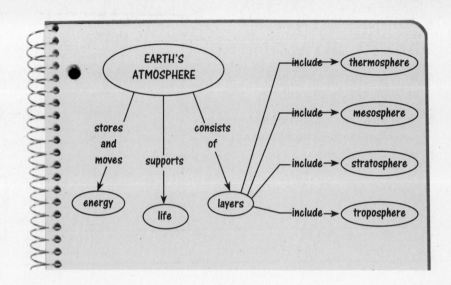

Venn Diagram

1 Draw two overlapping circles or ovals—one for each topic you are comparing—and label each one.

2 In the part of each circle that does not overlap with the other, list the characteristics that are unique to each topic.

3 In the space where the two circles overlap, list the characteristics that the two topics have in common.

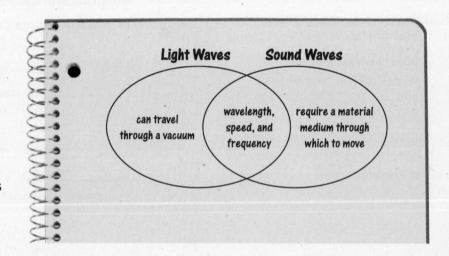

Cause-and-Effect Chart

1 Draw two boxes and connect them with an arrow.

2 In the first box, write the first event in a series (a cause).

3 In the second box, write a result of the cause (the effect).

4 Add more boxes when one event has many effects, or vice versa.

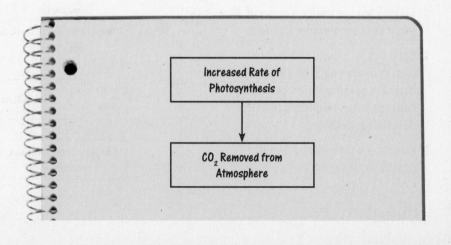

Process Diagram

A process can be a never-ending cycle. As you can see in this technology design process, engineers may backtrack and repeat steps, they may skip steps entirely, or they may repeat the entire process before a useable design is achieved.

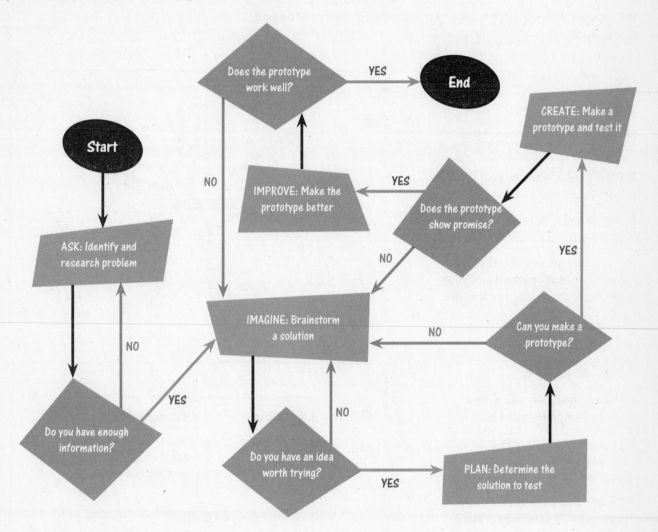

Reading and Study Skills

Using Vocabulary Strategies

Important science terms are highlighted where they are first defined in this book. One way to remember these terms is to take notes and make sketches when you come to them. Use the strategies on this page and the next for this purpose. You will also find a formal definition of each science term in the Glossary at the end of the book.

Description Wheel

1 Draw a small circle.

2 Write a vocabulary term inside the circle.

3 Draw several arms extending from the circle.

4 On the arms, write words and phrases that describe the term.

5 If you choose, add sketches that help you visualize the descriptive details or the concept as a whole.

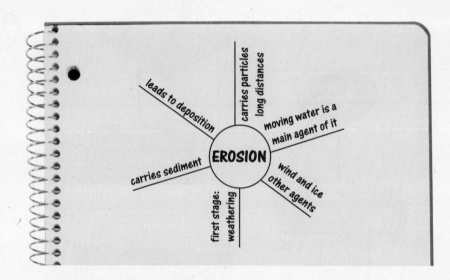

Four Square

1 Draw a small oval and write a vocabulary term inside it.

2 Draw a large rectangle around the oval, and divide the rectangle into four smaller squares.

3 Label the smaller squares with categories of information about the term, such as: definition, characteristics, examples, non-examples, appearance, and root words.

4 Fill the squares with descriptive words and drawings that will help you remember the overall meaning of the term and its essential details.

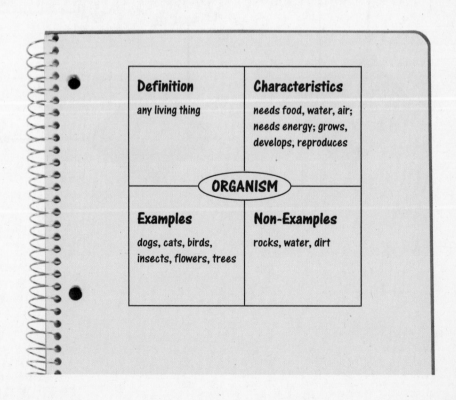

Frame Game

1 Draw a small rectangle, and write a vocabulary term inside it.

2 Draw a larger rectangle around the smaller one. Connect the corners of the larger rectangle to the corners of the smaller one, creating four spaces that frame the word.

3 In each of the four parts of the frame, draw or write details that help define the term. Consider including a definition, essential characteristics, an equation, examples, and a sentence using the term.

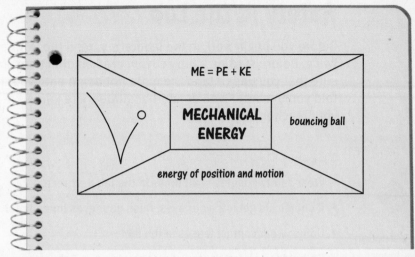

Magnet Word

1 Draw horseshoe magnet, and write a vocabulary term inside it.

2 Add lines that extend from the sides of the magnet.

3 Brainstorm words and phrases that come to mind when you think about the term.

4 On the lines, write the words and phrases that describe something essential about the term.

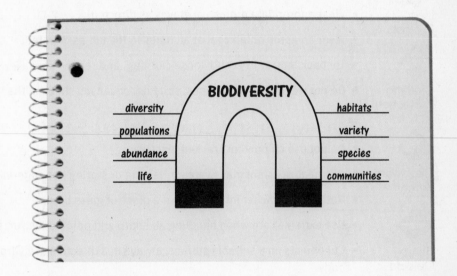

Word Triangle

1 Draw a triangle, and add lines to divide it into three parts.

2 Write a term and its definition in the bottom section of the triangle.

3 In the middle section, write a sentence in which the term is used correctly.

4 In the top section, draw a small picture to illustrate the term.

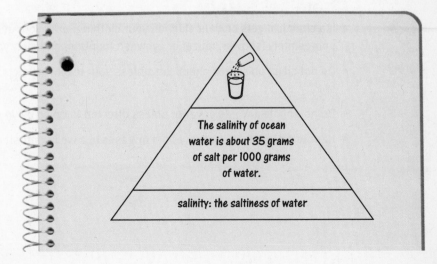

Science Skills

Safety in the Lab

Before you begin work in the laboratory, read these safety rules twice. Before starting a lab activity, read all directions and make sure that you understand them. Do not begin until your teacher has told you to start. If you or another student are injured in any way, tell your teacher immediately.

Dress Code

Eye Protection

- Wear safety goggles at all times in the lab as directed.
- If chemicals get into your eyes, flush your eyes immediately.
- Do not wear contact lenses in the lab.
- Do not look directly at the sun or any intense light source or laser.

Hand Protection

- Do not cut an object while holding the object in your hand.
- Wear appropriate protective gloves as directed.
- Wear an apron or lab coat at all times in the lab as directed.

Clothing Protection

- Tie back long hair, secure loose clothing, and remove loose jewelry.
- Do not wear open-toed shoes, sandals, or canvas shoes in the lab.

Glassware and Sharp Object Safety

Glassware Safety

- Do not use chipped or cracked glassware.
- Use heat-resistant glassware for heating or storing hot materials.
- Notify your teacher immediately if a piece of glass breaks.

Sharp Objects Safety

- Use extreme care when handling all sharp and pointed instruments.
- Cut objects on a suitable surface, always in a direction away from your body.

Chemical Safety

Chemical Safety

- If a chemical gets on your skin, on your clothing, or in your eyes, rinse it immediately (shower, faucet or eyewash fountain) and alert your teacher.
- Do not clean up spilled chemicals unless your teacher directs you to do so.
- Do not inhale any gas or vapor unless directed to do so by your teacher.
- Handle materials that emit vapors or gases in a well-ventilated area.

Electrical Safety

Electrical Safety

- Do not use equipment with frayed electrical cords or loose plugs.
- Do not use electrical equipment near water or when clothing or hands are wet.
- Hold the plug housing when you plug in or unplug equipment.

Heating and Fire Safety

Heating Safety

- Be aware of any source of flames, sparks, or heat (such as flames, heating coils, or hot plates) before working with any flammable substances.
- Know the location of lab fire extinguishers and fire-safety blankets.
- Know your school's fire-evacuation routes.
- If your clothing catches on fire, walk to the lab shower to put out the fire.
- Never leave a hot plate unattended while it is turned on or while it is cooling.
- Use tongs or appropriate insulated holders when handling heated objects.
- Allow all equipment to cool before storing it.

Wafting

Plant and Animal Safety

Plant Safety

Animal Safety

- Do not eat any part of a plant.
- Do not pick any wild plants unless your teacher instructs you to do so.
- Handle animals only as your teacher directs.
- Treat animals carefully and respectfully.
- Wash your hands thoroughly after handling any plant or animal.

Cleanup

Proper Waste Disposal

- Clean all work surfaces and protective equipment as directed by your teacher.
- Dispose of hazardous materials or sharp objects only as directed by your teacher.
- Keep your hands away from your face while you are working on any activity.
- Wash your hands thoroughly before you leave the lab or after any activity.

Hygienic Care

Science Skills

Designing, Conducting, and Reporting an Experiment

An experiment is an organized procedure to study something under specific conditions. Use the following steps of the scientific method when designing or conducting a controlled experiment.

1 Identify a Research Problem

Every day, you make observations by using your senses to gather information. Careful observations lead to good questions, and good questions can lead you to an experiment. Imagine, for example, that you pass a pond every day on your way to school, and you notice green scum beginning to form on top of it. You wonder what it is and why it seems to be growing. You list your questions, and then you do a little research to find out what is already known. A good place to start a research project is at the library. A library catalog lists all of the resources available to you at that library and often those found elsewhere. Begin your search by using:

- keywords or main topics.

- similar words, or synonyms, of your keyword.

The types of resources that will be helpful to you will depend on the kind of information you are interested in. And, some resources are more reliable for a given topic than others. Some different kinds of useful resources are:

- magazines and journals (or periodicals)—articles on a topic.

- encyclopedias—a good overview of a topic.

- books on specific subjects—details about a topic.

- newspapers—useful for current events.

The Internet can also be a great place to find information. Some of your library's reference materials may even be online. When using the Internet, however, it is especially important to make sure you are using appropriate and reliable sources. Websites of universities and government agencies are usually more accurate and reliable than websites created by individuals or businesses. Decide which sources are relevant and reliable for your topic. If in doubt, check with your teacher.

Take notes as you read through the information in these resources. You will probably come up with many questions and ideas for which you can do more research as needed. Once you feel you have enough information, think about the questions you have on the topic. Then, write down the problem that you want to investigate. Your notes might look like these.

© Houghton Mifflin Harcourt Publishing Company

Research Questions	Research Problem	Library and Internet Resources
• How do algae grow? • How do people measure algae? • What kind of fertilizer would affect the growth of algae? • Can fertilizer and algae be used safely in a lab? How?	How does fertilizer affect the algae in a pond?	Pond fertilization: initiating an algal bloom – from University of California Davis website. Blue-Green algae in Wisconsin waters-from the Department of Natural Resources of Wisconsin website.

As you gather information from reliable sources, record details about each source, including author name(s), title, date of publication, and/or web address. Make sure to also note the specific information that you use from each source. Staying organized in this way will be important when you write your report and create a bibliography or works cited list. Recording this information and staying organized will help you credit the appropriate author(s) for the information that you have gathered.

Representing someone else's ideas or work as your own, (without giving the original author credit), is known as plagiarism. Plagiarism can be intentional or unintentional. The best way to make sure that you do not commit plagiarism is to always do your own work and to always give credit to others when you use their words or ideas.

Current scientific research is built on scientific research and discoveries that have happened in the past. This means that scientists are constantly learning from each other and combining ideas to learn more about the natural world through investigation. But, a good scientist always credits the ideas and research that they have gathered from other people to those people. There are more details about crediting sources and creating a bibliography under step 9.

2 Make a Prediction

A prediction is a statement of what you expect will happen in your experiment. Before making a prediction, you need to decide in a general way what you will do in your procedure. You may state your prediction in an if-then format.

Prediction

If the amount of fertilizer in the pond water is increased, then the amount of algae will also increase.

Science Skills

3 Form a Hypothesis

Many experiments are designed to test a hypothesis. A hypothesis is a tentative explanation for an expected result. You have predicted that additional fertilizer will cause additional algae growth in pond water; your hypothesis should state the connection between fertilizer and algal growth.

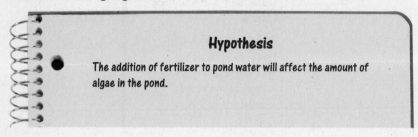

Hypothesis

The addition of fertilizer to pond water will affect the amount of algae in the pond.

4 Identify Variables to Test the Hypothesis

The next step is to design an experiment to test the hypothesis. The experimental results may or may not support the hypothesis. Either way, the information that results from the experiment may be useful for future investigations.

Experimental Group and Control Group

An experiment to determine how two factors are related has a control group and an experimental group. The two groups are the same, except that the investigator changes a single factor in the experimental group and does not change it in the control group.

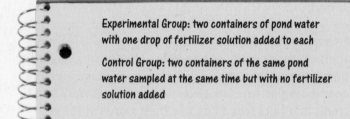

Experimental Group: two containers of pond water with one drop of fertilizer solution added to each

Control Group: two containers of the same pond water sampled at the same time but with no fertilizer solution added

Variables and Constants

In a controlled experiment, a variable is any factor that can change. Constants are all of the variables that are kept the same in both the experimental group and the control group.

The independent variable is the factor that is manipulated or changed in order to test the effect of the change on another variable. The dependent variable is the factor the investigator measures to gather data about the effect.

Independent Variable	Dependent Variable	Constants
Amount of fertilizer in pond water	Growth of algae in the pond water	• Where and when the pond water is obtained • The type of container used • Light and temperature conditions where the water is stored

5 Write a Procedure

Write each step of your procedure. Start each step with a verb, or action word, and keep the steps short. Your procedure should be clear enough for someone else to use as instructions for repeating your experiment.

Procedure

1. Use the masking tape and the marker to label the containers with your initials, the date, and the identifiers "Jar 1 with Fertilizer," "Jar 2 with Fertilizer," "Jar 1 without Fertilizer," and "Jar 2 without Fertilizer."

2. Put on your gloves. Use the large container to obtain a sample of pond water.

3. Divide the water sample equally among the four smaller containers.

4. Use the eyedropper to add one drop of fertilizer solution to the two containers labeled, "Jar 1 with Fertilizer," and "Jar 2 with Fertilizer".

5. Cover the containers with clear plastic wrap. Use the scissors to punch ten holes in each of the covers.

6. Place all four containers on a window ledge. Make sure that they all receive the same amount of light.

7. Observe the containers every day for one week.

8. Use the ruler to measure the diameter of the largest clump of algae in each container, and record your measurements daily.

Science Skills

6 Experiment and Collect Data

Once you have all of your materials and your procedure has been approved, you can begin to experiment and collect data. Record both quantitative data (measurements) and qualitative data (observations), as shown below.

Algal Growth and Fertilizer

Date and Time	Experimental Group		Control Group		Observations
	Jar 1 with Fertilizer (diameter of algal clump in mm)	Jar 2 with Fertilizer (diameter of algal clump in mm)	Jar 1 without Fertilizer (diameter of algal clump in mm)	Jar 2 without Fertilizer (diameter of algal clump in mm)	
5/3 4:00 p.m.	0	0	0	0	condensation in all containers
5/4 4:00 p.m.	0	3	0	0	tiny green blobs in Jar 2 with fertilizer
5/5 4:15 p.m.	4	5	0	3	green blobs in Jars 1 and 2 with fertilizer and Jar 2 without fertilizer
5/6 4:00 p.m.	5	6	0	4	water light green in Jar 2 with fertilizer
5/7 4:00 p.m.	8	10	0	6	water light green in Jars 1 and 2 with fertilizer and Jar 2 without fertilizer
5/8 3:30 p.m.	10	18	0	6	cover off of Jar 2 with fertilizer
5/9 3:30 p.m.	14	23	0	8	drew sketches of each container

Drawings of Samples Viewed Under Microscope on 5/9 at 100x

Jar 1 with Fertilizer

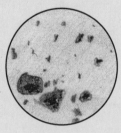

Jar 2 with Fertilizer

Jar 1 without Fertilizer

Jar 2 without Fertilizer

7 Analyze Data

After you complete your experiment, you must analyze all of the data you have gathered. Tables, statistics, and graphs are often used in this step to organize and analyze both the qualitative and quantitative data. Sometimes, your qualitative data are best used to help explain the relationships you see in your quantitative data.

Computer graphing software is useful for creating a graph from data that you have collected. Most graphing software can make line graphs, pie charts, or bar graphs from data that has been organized in a spreadsheet. Graphs are useful for understanding relationships in the data and for communicating the results of your experiment.

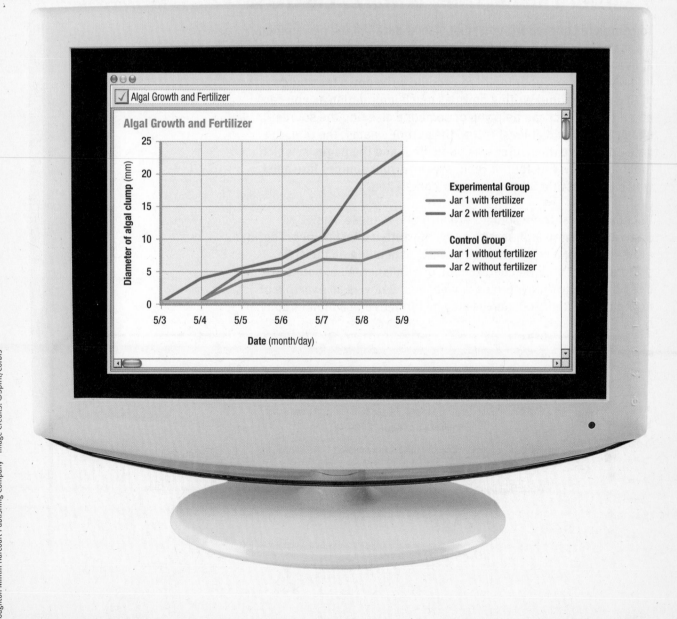

8 Make Conclusions

To draw conclusions from your experiment, first, write your results. Then, compare your results with your hypothesis. Do your results support your hypothesis? What have you learned?

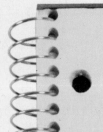

Conclusion

More algae grew in the pond water to which fertilizer had been added than in the pond water to which fertilizer had not been added. My hypothesis was supported. I conclude that it is possible that the growth of algae in ponds can be influenced by the input of fertilizer.

9 Create a Bibliography or Works Cited List

To complete your report, you must also show all of the newspapers, magazines, journals, books, and online sources that you used at every stage of your investigation. Whenever you find useful information about your topic, you should write down the source of that information. Writing down as much information as you can about the subject can help you or someone else find the source again. You should at least record the author's name, the title, the date and where the source was published, and the pages in which the information was found. Then, organize your sources into a list, which you can title Bibliography or Works Cited.

Usually, at least three sources are included in these lists. Sources are listed alphabetically, by the authors' last names. The exact format of a bibliography can vary, depending on the style preferences of your teacher, school, or publisher. Also, books are cited differently than journals or websites. Below is an example of how different kinds of sources may be formatted in a bibliography.

BOOK: Hauschultz, Sara. Freshwater Algae. Brainard, Minnesota: Northwoods Publishing, 2011.

ENCYCLOPEDIA: Lasure, Sedona. "Algae is not all just pond scum." Encyclopedia of Algae. 2009.

JOURNAL: Johnson, Keagan. "Algae as we know it." Sci Journal, vol 64. (September 2010): 201-211.

WEBSITE: Dout, Bill. "Keeping algae scum out of birdbaths." Help Keep Earth Clean. News. January 26, 2011. <www.SaveEarth.org>.

Using a Microscope

Scientists use microscopes to see very small objects that cannot easily be seen with the eye alone. A microscope magnifies the image of an object so that small details may be observed. A microscope that you may use can magnify an object 400 times—the object will appear 400 times larger than its actual size.

Eyepiece Objects are viewed through the eyepiece. The eyepiece contains a lens that commonly magnifies an image ten times.

Body The body separates the lens in the eyepiece from the objective lenses below.

Coarse Adjustment This knob is used to focus the image of an object when it is viewed through the low-power lens.

Nosepiece The nosepiece holds the objective lenses above the stage and rotates so that all lenses may be used.

Fine Adjustment This knob is used to focus the image of an object when it is viewed through the high-power lens.

High-Power Objective Lens This is the largest lens on the nosepiece. It magnifies an image approximately 40 times.

Low-Power Objective Lens This is the smallest lens on the nosepiece. It magnifies images about 10 times.

Stage The stage supports the object being viewed.

Arm The arm supports the body above the stage. Always carry a microscope by the arm and base.

Diaphragm The diaphragm is used to adjust the amount of light passing through the slide and into an objective lens.

Stage Clip The stage clip holds a slide in place on the stage.

Mirror or Light Source Some microscopes use light that is reflected through the stage by a mirror. Other microscopes have their own light sources.

Base The base supports the microscope.

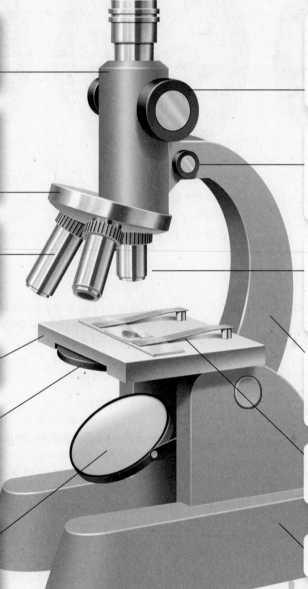

Science Skills

Measuring Accurately

Precision and Accuracy

When you do a scientific investigation, it is important that your methods, observations, and data be both precise and accurate.

Low precision: The darts did not land in a consistent place on the dartboard.

Precision, but not accuracy: The darts landed in a consistent place, but did not hit the bull's eye.

Prescision and accuracy: The darts landed consistently on the bull's eye.

Precision

In science, *precision* is the exactness and consistency of measurements. For example, measurements made with a ruler that has both centimeter and millimeter markings would be more precise than measurements made with a ruler that has only centimeter markings. Another indicator of precision is the care taken to make sure that methods and observations are as exact and consistent as possible. Every time a particular experiment is done, the same procedure should be used. Precision is necessary because experiments are repeated several times and if the procedure changes, the results might change.

Example

Suppose you are measuring temperatures over a two-week period. Your precision will be greater if you measure each temperature at the same place, at the same time of day, and with the same thermometer than if you change any of these factors from one day to the next.

Accuracy

In science, it is possible to be precise but not accurate. *Accuracy* depends on the difference between a measurement and an actual value. The smaller the difference, the more accurate the measurement.

Example

Suppose you look at a stream and estimate that it is about 1 meter wide at a particular place. You decide to check your estimate by measuring the stream with a meter stick, and you determine that the stream is 1.32 meters wide. However, because it is difficult to measure the width of a stream with a meter stick, it turns out that your measurement was not very accurate. The stream is actually 1.14 meters wide. Therefore, even though your estimate of about 1 meter was less precise than your measurement, your estimate was actually more accurate.

Graduated Cylinders

How to Measure the Volume of a Liquid with a Graduated Cylinder

- Be sure that the graduated cylinder is on a flat surface so that your measurement will be accurate.

- When reading the scale on a graduated cylinder, be sure to have your eyes at the level of the surface of the liquid.

- The surface of the liquid will be curved in the graduated cylinder. Read the volume of the liquid at the bottom of the curve, or meniscus (muh-NIHS-kuhs).

- You can use a graduated cylinder to find the volume of a solid object by measuring the increase in a liquid's level after you add the object to the cylinder.

meniscus

Read the volume at the bottom of the meniscus. The volume is 96 mL.

Metric Rulers

How to Measure the Length of a Leaf with a Metric Ruler

1 Lay a ruler flat on top of the leaf so that the 1-centimeter mark lines up with one end. Make sure the ruler and the leaf do not move between the time you line them up and the time you take the measurement.

2 Look straight down on the ruler so that you can see exactly how the marks line up with the other end of the leaf.

3 Estimate the length by which the leaf extends beyond a marking. For example, the leaf below extends about halfway between the 4.2-centimeter and 4.3-centimeter marks, so the apparent measurement is about 4.25 centimeters.

4 Remember to subtract 1 centimeter from your apparent measurement, since you started at the 1-centimeter mark on the ruler and not at the end. The leaf is about 3.25 centimeters long (4.25 cm − 1 cm = 3.25 cm).

Triple Beam Balance

This balance has a pan and three beams with sliding masses, called riders. At one end of the beams is a pointer that indicates whether the mass on the pan is equal to the masses shown on the beams.

How to Measure the Mass of an Object

1 Make sure the balance is zeroed before measuring the mass of an object. The balance is zeroed if the pointer is at zero when nothing is on the pan and the riders are at their zero points. Use the adjustment knob at the base of the balance to zero it.

2 Place the object to be measured on the pan.

3 Move the riders one notch at a time away from the pan. Begin with the largest rider. If moving the largest rider one notch brings the pointer below zero, begin measuring the mass of the object with the next smaller rider.

4 Change the positions of the riders until they balance the mass on the pan and the pointer is at zero. Then add the readings from the three beams to determine the mass of the object.

300 g	position of largest rider
90 g	position of middle rider
+ 3 g	position of smallest rider
393 g	mass of beaker and water

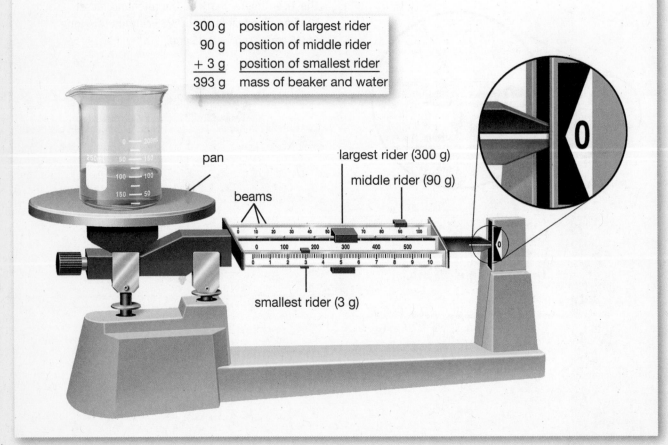

pan

beams

largest rider (300 g)

middle rider (90 g)

smallest rider (3 g)

Using the Metric System and SI Units

Scientists use International System (SI) units for measurements of distance, volume, mass, and temperature. The International System is based on powers of ten and the metric system of measurement.

Basic SI Units		
Quantity	**Name**	**Symbol**
length	meter	m
volume	liter	L
mass	gram	g
temperature	kelvin	K

SI Prefixes		
Prefix	**Symbol**	**Power of 10**
kilo-	k	1000
hecto-	h	100
deca-	da	10
deci-	d	0.1 or $\frac{1}{10}$
centi-	c	0.01 or $\frac{1}{100}$
milli-	m	0.001 or $\frac{1}{1000}$

Changing Metric Units

You can change from one unit to another in the metric system by multiplying or dividing by a power of 10.

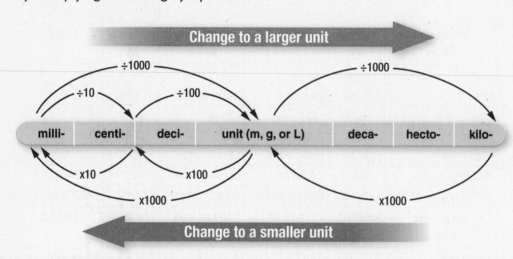

Example

Change 0.64 liters to milliliters.
  1 Decide whether to multiply or divide.
  2 Select the power of 10.

Change to a smaller unit by multiplying

mL ◄─── x 1000 ─── L

0.64 x 1000 = 640.

ANSWER 0.64 L = 640 mL

Example

Change 23.6 grams to kilograms.
  1 Decide whether to multiply or divide.
  2 Select the power of 10.

Change to a larger unit by dividing

g ─── ÷ 1000 ──► kg

26.3 ÷ 1000 = 0.0263

ANSWER 23.6 g = 0.0236 kg

Science Skills

Converting Between SI and U.S. Customary Units

Use the chart below when you need to convert between SI units and U.S. customary units.

SI Unit	From SI to U.S. Customary			From U.S. Customary to SI		
Length	**When you know**	**multiply by**	**to find**	**When you know**	**multiply by**	**to find**
kilometer (km) = 1000 m	kilometers	0.62	miles	miles	1.61	kilometers
meter (m) = 100 cm	meters	3.28	feet	feet	0.3048	meters
centimeter (cm) = 10 mm	centimeters	0.39	inches	inches	2.54	centimeters
millimeter (mm) = 0.1 cm	millimeters	0.04	inches	inches	25.4	millimeters
Area	**When you know**	**multiply by**	**to find**	**When you know**	**multiply by**	**to find**
square kilometer (km²)	square kilometers	0.39	square miles	square miles	2.59	square kilometers
square meter (m²)	square meters	1.2	square yards	square yards	0.84	square meters
square centimeter (cm²)	square centimeters	0.155	square inches	square inches	6.45	square centimeters
Volume	**When you know**	**multiply by**	**to find**	**When you know**	**multiply by**	**to find**
liter (L) = 1000 mL	liters	1.06	quarts	quarts	0.95	liters
	liters	0.26	gallons	gallons	3.79	liters
	liters	4.23	cups	cups	0.24	liters
	liters	2.12	pints	pints	0.47	liters
milliliter (mL) = 0.001 L	milliliters	0.20	teaspoons	teaspoons	4.93	milliliters
	milliliters	0.07	tablespoons	tablespoons	14.79	milliliters
	milliliters	0.03	fluid ounces	fluid ounces	29.57	milliliters
Mass	**When you know**	**multiply by**	**to find**	**When you know**	**multiply by**	**to find**
kilogram (kg) = 1000 g	kilograms	2.2	pounds	pounds	0.45	kilograms
gram (g) = 1000 mg	grams	0.035	ounces	ounces	28.35	grams

Temperature Conversions

Even though the kelvin is the SI base unit of temperature, the degree Celsius will be the unit you use most often in your science studies. The formulas below show the relationships between temperatures in degrees Fahrenheit (°F), degrees Celsius (°C), and kelvins (K).

$$°C = \frac{5}{9}\,(°F - 32) \qquad °F = \frac{9}{5}\,°C + 32 \qquad K = °C + 273$$

Examples of Temperature Conversions

Condition	Degrees Celsius	Degrees Fahrenheit
Freezing point of water	0	32
Cool day	10	50
Mild day	20	68
Warm day	30	86
Normal body temperature	37	98.6
Very hot day	40	104
Boiling point of water	100	212

Math Refresher

Performing Calculations

Science requires an understanding of many math concepts. The following pages will help you review some important math skills.

Mean

The mean is the sum of all values in a data set divided by the total number of values in the data set. The mean is also called the *average*.

Example

Find the mean of the following set of numbers: 5, 4, 7, and 8.

Step 1   Find the sum.

$5 + 4 + 7 + 8 = 24$

Step 2   Divide the sum by the number of numbers in your set. Because there are four numbers in this example, divide the sum by 4.

$24 \div 4 = 6$

Answer The average, or mean, is 6.

Median

The median of a data set is the middle value when the values are written in numerical order. If a data set has an even number of values, the median is the mean of the two middle values.

Example

To find the median of a set of measurements, arrange the values in order from least to greatest. The median is the middle value.

13 mm   14 mm   16 mm   21 mm   23 mm

Answer The median is 16 mm.

Mode

The mode of a data set is the value that occurs most often.

Example

To find the mode of a set of measurements, arrange the values in order from least to greatest and determine the value that occurs most often.

13 mm, 14 mm, 14 mm, 16 mm, 21 mm, 23 mm, 25 mm

Answer The mode is 14 mm.

A data set can have more than one mode or no mode. For example, the following data set has modes of 2 mm and 4 mm:

2 mm   2 mm   3 mm   4 mm   4 mm

The data set below has no mode, because no value occurs more often than any other.

2 mm   3 mm   4 mm   5 mm

Math Refresher

Ratios

A **ratio** is a comparison between numbers, and it is usually written as a fraction.

Example

Find the ratio of thermometers to students if you have 36 thermometers and 48 students in your class.

Step 1 Write the ratio.

$$\frac{36 \text{ thermometers}}{48 \text{ students}}$$

Step 2 Simplify the fraction to its simplest form.

$$\frac{36}{48} = \frac{36 \div 12}{48 \div 12} = \frac{3}{4}$$

The ratio of thermometers to students is 3 to 4 or 3:4.

Proportions

A **proportion** is an equation that states that two ratios are equal.

$$\frac{3}{1} = \frac{12}{4}$$

To solve a proportion, you can use cross-multiplication. If you know three of the quantities in a proportion, you can use cross-multiplication to find the fourth.

Example

Imagine that you are making a scale model of the solar system for your science project. The diameter of Jupiter is 11.2 times the diameter of the Earth. If you are using a plastic-foam ball that has a diameter of 2 cm to represent the Earth, what must the diameter of the ball representing Jupiter be?

$$\frac{11.2}{1} = \frac{x}{2 \text{ cm}}$$

Step 1 Cross-multiply.

$$\frac{11.2}{1} = \frac{x}{2}$$

$$11.2 \times 2 = x \times 1$$

Step 2 Multiply.

$$22.4 = x \times 1$$

$$x = 22.4 \text{ cm}$$

You will need to use a ball that has a diameter of 22.4 cm to represent Jupiter.

Rates

A **rate** is a ratio of two values expressed in different units. A unit rate is a rate with a denominator of 1 unit.

Example

A plant grew 6 centimeters in 2 days. The plant's rate of growth was $\frac{6 \text{ cm}}{2 \text{ days}}$.
To describe the plant's growth in centimeters per day, write a unit rate.

Divide numerator and denominator by 2:

$$\frac{6 \text{ cm}}{2 \text{ days}} = \frac{6 \text{ cm} \div 2}{2 \text{ days} \div 2}$$

Simplify:

$$= \frac{3 \text{ cm}}{1 \text{ day}}$$

Answer The plant's rate of growth is 3 centimeters per day.

Percent

A **percent** is a ratio of a given number to 100. For example, 85% = 85/100. You can use percent to find part of a whole.

Example
What is 85% of 40?

Step 1 Rewrite the percent as a decimal by moving the decimal point two places to the left.

$$0.85$$

Step 2 Multiply the decimal by the number that you are calculating the percentage of.

$$0.85 \times 40 = 34$$

85% of 40 is 34.

Decimals

To **add** or **subtract decimals**, line up the digits vertically so that the decimal points line up. Then, add or subtract the columns from right to left. Carry or borrow numbers as necessary.

Example
Add the following numbers: 3.1415 and 2.96.

Step 1 Line up the digits vertically so that the decimal points line up.

$$\begin{array}{r} 3.1415 \\ + 2.96 \\ \hline \end{array}$$

Step 2 Add the columns from right to left, and carry when necessary.

$$\begin{array}{r} 3.1415 \\ + 2.96 \\ \hline 6.1015 \end{array}$$

The sum is 6.1015.

Fractions

A **fraction** is a ratio of two nonzero whole numbers.

Example
Your class has 24 plants. Your teacher instructs you to put 5 plants in a shady spot. What fraction of the plants in your class will you put in a shady spot?

Step 1 In the denominator, write the total number of parts in the whole.

$$\frac{?}{24}$$

Step 2 In the numerator, write the number of parts of the whole that are being considered.

$$\frac{5}{24}$$

So, $\frac{5}{24}$ of the plants will be in the shade.

Math Refresher

Simplifying Fractions

It is usually best to express a fraction in its simplest form. Expressing a fraction in its simplest form is called **simplifying a fraction**.

Example

Simplify the fraction $\frac{30}{45}$ to its simplest form.

Step 1   Find the largest whole number that will divide evenly into both the numerator and denominator. This number is called the greatest common factor (GCF).

Factors of the numerator 30:
1, 2, 3, 5, 6, 10, 15, 30

Factors of the denominator 45:
1, 3, 5, 9, 15, 45

Step 2   Divide both the numerator and the denominator by the GCF, which in this case is 15.

$$\frac{30}{45} = \frac{30 \div 15}{45 \div 15} = \frac{2}{3}$$

Thus, $\frac{30}{45}$ written in its simplest form is $\frac{2}{3}$.

Adding and Subtracting Fractions

To **add** or **subtract fractions** that have the same denominator, simply add or subtract the numerators.

Examples

$\frac{3}{5} + \frac{1}{5} = ?$ and $\frac{3}{4} - \frac{1}{4} = ?$

Step 1   Add or subtract the numerators.

$$\frac{3}{5} + \frac{1}{5} = \frac{4}{} \text{ and } \frac{3}{4} - \frac{1}{4} = \frac{2}{}$$

Step 2   Write in the common denominator, which remains the same.

$$\frac{3}{5} + \frac{1}{5} = \frac{4}{5} \text{ and } \frac{3}{4} - \frac{1}{4} = \frac{2}{4}$$

Step 3   If necessary, write the fraction in its simplest form.

$\frac{4}{5}$ cannot be simplified, and $\frac{2}{4} = \frac{1}{2}$.

To **add** or **subtract** fractions that have **different denominators,** first find the least common denominator (LCD).

Examples

$\frac{1}{2} + \frac{1}{6} = ?$ and $\frac{3}{4} - \frac{2}{3} = ?$

Step 1   Write the equivalent fractions that have a common denominator.

$$\frac{3}{6} + \frac{1}{6} = ? \text{ and } \frac{9}{12} - \frac{8}{12} = ?$$

Step 2   Add or subtract the fractions.

$$\frac{3}{6} + \frac{1}{6} = \frac{4}{6} \text{ and } \frac{9}{12} - \frac{8}{12} = \frac{1}{12}$$

Step 3   If necessary, write the fraction in its simplest form.

$\frac{4}{6} = \frac{2}{3}$, and $\frac{1}{12}$ cannot be simplifed.

Multiplying Fractions

To **multiply fractions**, multiply the numerators and the denominators together, and then simplify the fraction to its simplest form.

Example

$\frac{5}{9} \times \frac{7}{10} = ?$

Step 1   Multiply the numerators and denominators.

$$\frac{5}{9} \times \frac{7}{10} = \frac{5 \times 7}{9 \times 10} = \frac{35}{90}$$

Step 2   Simplify the fraction.

$$\frac{35}{90} = \frac{35 \div 5}{90 \div 5} = \frac{7}{18}$$

Dividing Fractions

To **divide fractions**, first rewrite the divisor (the number you divide by) upside down. This number is called the reciprocal of the divisor. Then multiply and simplify if necessary.

Example

$$\frac{5}{8} \div \frac{3}{2} = ?$$

Step 1   Rewrite the divisor as its reciprocal.

$$\frac{3}{2} \rightarrow \frac{2}{3}$$

Step 2   Multiply the fractions.

$$\frac{5}{8} \times \frac{2}{3} = \frac{5 \times 2}{8 \times 3} = \frac{10}{24}$$

Step 3   Simplify the fraction.

$$\frac{10}{24} = \frac{10 \div 2}{24 \div 2} = \frac{5}{12}$$

Using Significant Figures

The **significant figures** in a decimal are the digits that are warranted by the accuracy of a measuring device.

When you perform a calculation with measurements, the number of significant figures to include in the result depends in part on the number of significant figures in the measurements. When you multiply or divide measurements, your answer should have only as many significant figures as the measurement with the fewest significant figures.

Examples

Using a balance and a graduated cylinder filled with water, you determined that a marble has a mass of 8.0 grams and a volume of 3.5 cubic centimeters. To calculate the density of the marble, divide the mass by the volume.

Write the formula for density: $\text{Density} = \dfrac{\text{mass}}{\text{volume}}$

Substitute measurements: $= \dfrac{8.0 \text{ g}}{3.5 \text{ cm}^3}$

Use a calculator to divide: $\approx 2.285714286 \text{ g/cm}^3$

Answer Because the mass and the volume have two significant figures each, give the density to two significant figures. The marble has a density of 2.3 grams per cubic centimeter.

Using Scientific Notation

Scientific notation is a shorthand way to write very large or very small numbers. For example, 73,500,000,000,000,000,000,000 kg is the mass of the moon. In scientific notation, it is 7.35×10^{22} kg. A value written as a number between 1 and 10, times a power of 10, is in scientific notation.

Examples

You can convert from standard form to scientific notation.

Standard Form	Scientific Notation
720,000	7.2×10^5
5 decimal places left	Exponent is 5.
0.000291	2.91×10^{-4}
4 decimal places right	Exponent is −4.

You can convert from scientific notation to standard form.

Scientific Notation	Standard Form
4.63×10^7	46,300,000
Exponent is 7.	7 decimal places right
1.08×10^{-6}	0.00000108
Exponent is −6.	6 decimal places left

Math Refresher

Making and Interpreting Graphs

Circle Graph

A circle graph, or pie chart, shows how each group of data relates to all of the data. Each part of the circle represents a category of the data. The entire circle represents all of the data. For example, a biologist studying a hardwood forest in Wisconsin found that there were five different types of trees. The data table at right summarizes the biologist's findings.

Wisconsin Hardwood Trees	
Type of tree	**Number found**
Oak	600
Maple	750
Beech	300
Birch	1,200
Hickory	150
Total	3,000

How to Make a Circle Graph

1 To make a circle graph of these data, first find the percentage of each type of tree. Divide the number of trees of each type by the total number of trees, and multiply by 100%.

$$\frac{600 \text{ oak}}{3,000 \text{ trees}} \times 100\% = 20\%$$

$$\frac{750 \text{ maple}}{3,000 \text{ trees}} \times 100\% = 25\%$$

$$\frac{300 \text{ beech}}{3,000 \text{ trees}} \times 100\% = 10\%$$

$$\frac{1,200 \text{ birch}}{3,000 \text{ trees}} \times 100\% = 40\%$$

$$\frac{150 \text{ hickory}}{3,000 \text{ trees}} \times 100\% = 5\%$$

2 Now, determine the size of the wedges that make up the graph. Multiply each percentage by 360°. Remember that a circle contains 360°.

$$20\% \times 360° = 72° \qquad 25\% \times 360° = 90°$$

$$10\% \times 360° = 36° \qquad 40\% \times 360° = 144°$$

$$5\% \times 360° = 18°$$

3 Check that the sum of the percentages is 100 and the sum of the degrees is 360.

$$20\% + 25\% + 10\% + 40\% + 5\% = 100\%$$

$$72° + 90° + 36° + 144° + 18° = 360°$$

4 Use a compass to draw a circle and mark the center of the circle.

5 Then, use a protractor to draw angles of 72°, 90°, 36°, 144°, and 18° in the circle.

6 Finally, label each part of the graph, and choose an appropriate title.

A Community of Wisconsin Hardwood Trees

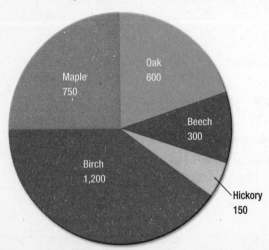

Line Graphs

Line graphs are most often used to demonstrate continuous change. For example, Mr. Smith's students analyzed the population records for their hometown, Appleton, between 1910 and 2010. Examine the data at right.

    Because the year and the population change, they are the variables. The population is determined by, or dependent on, the year. Therefore, the population is called the **dependent variable,** and the year is called the **independent variable**. Each year and its population make a **data pair**. To prepare a line graph, you must first organize data pairs into a table like the one at right.

Population of Appleton, 1910–2010	
Year	**Population**
1910	1,800
1930	2,500
1950	3,200
1970	3,900
1990	4,600
2010	5,300

How to Make a Line Graph

1 Place the independent variable along the horizontal (*x*) axis. Place the dependent variable along the vertical (*y*) axis.

2 Label the *x*-axis "Year" and the *y*-axis "Population." Look at your greatest and least values for the population. For the *y*-axis, determine a scale that will provide enough space to show these values. You must use the same scale for the entire length of the axis. Next, find an appropriate scale for the *x*-axis.

3 Choose reasonable starting points for each axis.

4 Plot the data pairs as accurately as possible.

5 Choose a title that accurately represents the data.

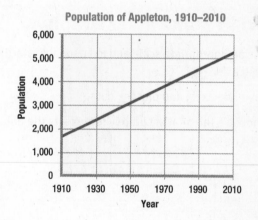

How to Determine Slope

Slope is the ratio of the change in the *y*-value to the change in the x-value, or "rise over run."

1 Choose two points on the line graph. For example, the population of Appleton in 2010 was 5,300 people. Therefore, you can define point A as (2010, 5,300). In 1910, the population was 1,800 people. You can define point B as (1910, 1,800).

2 Find the change in the *y*-value.
(*y* at point A) − (*y* at point B) =
5,300 people − 1,800 people =
3,500 people

3 Find the change in the *x*-value.
(*x* at point A) − (*x* at point B) =
2010 − 1910 = 100 years

4 Calculate the slope of the graph by dividing the change in *y* by the change in *x*.

$$slope = \frac{change\ in\ y}{change\ in\ x}$$

$$slope = \frac{3,500\ people}{100\ years}$$

$$slope = 35\ people\ per\ year$$

In this example, the population in Appleton increased by a fixed amount each year. The graph of these data is a straight line. Therefore, the relationship is **linear**. When the graph of a set of data is not a straight line, the relationship is **nonlinear**.

Math Refresher

Bar Graphs

Bar graphs can be used to demonstrate change that is not continuous. These graphs can be used to indicate trends when the data cover a long period of time. A meteorologist gathered the precipitation data shown here for Summerville for April 1–15 and used a bar graph to represent the data.

Precipitation in Summerville, April 1–15			
Date	Precipitation (cm)	Date	Precipitation (cm)
April 1	0.5	April 9	0.25
April 2	1.25	April 10	0.0
April 3	0.0	April 11	1.0
April 4	0.0	April 12	0.0
April 5	0.0	April 13	0.25
April 6	0.0	April 14	0.0
April 7	0.0	April 15	6.50
April 8	1.75		

How to Make a Bar Graph

1 Use an appropriate scale and a reasonable starting point for each axis.

2 Label the axes, and plot the data.

3 Choose a title that accurately represents the data.

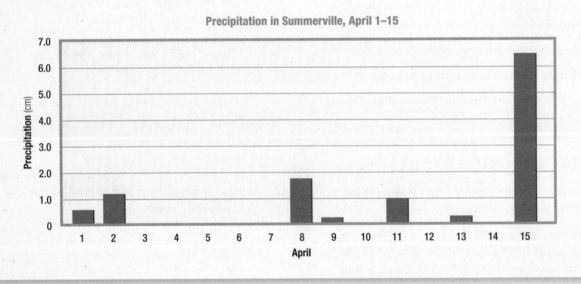

Precipitation in Summerville, April 1–15

Glossary

Pronunciation Key

Sound	Symbol	Example	Respelling	Sound	Symbol	Example	Respelling
ă	a	pat	PAT	ŏ	ah	bottle	BAHT'l
ā	ay	pay	PAY	ō	oh	toe	TOH
âr	air	care	KAIR	ô	aw	caught	KAWT
ä	ah	father	FAH•ther	ôr	ohr	roar	ROHR
är	ar	argue	AR•gyoo	oi	oy	noisy	NOYZ•ee
ch	ch	chase	CHAYS	o͝o	u	book	BUK
ĕ	e	pet	PET	o͞o	oo	boot	BOOT
ĕ (at end of a syllable)	eh	settee lessee	seh•TEE leh•SEE	ou	ow	pound	POWND
ĕr	ehr	merry	MEHR•ee	s	s	center	SEN•ter
ē	ee	beach	BEECH	sh	sh	cache	CASH
g	g	gas	GAS	ŭ	uh	flood	FLUHD
ĭ	i	pit	PIT	ûr	er	bird	BERD
ĭ (at end of a syllable)	ih	guitar	gih•TAR	z	z	xylophone	ZY•luh•fohn
ī	y eye (only for a complete syllable)	pie island	PY EYE•luhnd	z	z	bags	BAGZ
				zh	zh	decision	dih•SIZH•uhn
				ə	uh	around broken focus	uh•ROWND BROH•kuhn FOH•kuhs
îr	ir	hear	HIR	ər	er	winner	WIN•er
j	j	germ	JERM	th	th	thin they	THIN THAY
k	k	kick	KIK				
ng	ng	thing	THING	w	w	one	WUHN
ngk	ngk	bank	BANGK	wh	hw	whether	HWETH•er

absorption (uhb·SOHRP·shuhn) in optics, the transfer of light energy to particles of matter (97)

absorción en la óptica, la transferencia de energía luminosa a las partículas de materia

amplitude (AM·plih·tood) the maximum distance that the particles of a wave's medium vibrate from their rest position (18)

amplitud la distancia máxima a la que vibran las partículas del medio de una onda a partir de su posición de reposo

concave (kahn·KAYV) curved or rounded inward like the inside of a spoon (108)

cóncavo curvado o redondeado hacia adentro como la parte interior de una cuchara

converge (kuhn·VERJ) to come together; a converging lens or mirror causes parallel beams of light to come together at a single point (108)

convergir unirse; una lente o espejo convergente hace que los rayos de luz paralelos se unan en un mismo punto

convex (KAHN·veks) curved or rounded outward like the back of a spoon (109)

convexo curvado o redondeado hacia afuera como la parte exterior de una cuchara

cornea (KOHR·nee·uh) a transparent membrane that covers the iris and pupil of the eye; much of the eye's refraction occurs as light passes through the cornea (120)

córnea una membrana transparente que cubre el iris y la pupila del ojo; gran parte de la refracción del ojo ocurre cuando la luz pasa a través de la córnea

decibel (DES·uh·bel) the most common unit used to measure loudness (symbol, dB) (44)

decibele la unidad más común que se usa para medir el volumen del sonido (símbolo: dB)

diverge (dih·VERJ) to move apart; a diverging lens or mirror causes parallel beams of light to spread apart as if they came from a single point (109)

divergir separarse; una lente o espejo divergente hace que los rayos de luz paralelos se separen como si provinieran de un mismo punto

Doppler effect (DAHP·ler ih·FEKT) an observed change in the frequency of a wave when the source or observer is moving (45)

efecto Doppler un cambio que se observa en la frecuencia de una onda cuando la fuente o el observador está en movimiento

echo (EK·oh) a reflected sound wave (53)

eco una onda de sonido reflejada

echolocation (ek·oh·loh·KAY·shuhn) the process of using reflected sound waves to find objects; used by animals such as bats (64)

ecolocación el proceso de usar ondas de sonido reflejadas para buscar objetos; utilizado por animales tales como los murciélagos

electromagnetic spectrum (ee·lek·troh·mag·NET·ik SPEK·truhm) all of the frequencies or wavelengths of electromagnetic radiation (86)

espectro electromagnético todas las frecuencias o longitudes de onda de la radiación electromagnética

electromagnetic wave (ee·lek·troh·mag·NET·ik WAYV) a wave, consisting of changing electric and magnetic fields, that is emitted by vibrating electric charges and can travel through a vacuum (10)

onda electromagnética una onda formada por campos eléctricos y magnéticos cambiantes, que es emitida por cargas eléctricas que vibran, y que puede viajar por un vacío

fluorescent light (flu·RES·uhnt LYT) visible light emitted by a material when it absorbs energy such as ultraviolet light (128)

luz fluorescente luz visible emitida por un material cuando absorbe energía como la luz ultravioleta

frequency (FREE·kwuhn·see) the number of cycles, such as waves, in a given amount of time (19)

frecuencia el número de ciclos, tales como ondas, producidas en una determinada cantidad de tiempo

H

Hertz (HERTS) a unit of frequency equal to one cycle per second (19)

hertz una unidad de frecuencia que representa un ciclo por segundo

I–K

incandescent light (in·kuhn·DES·uhnt LYT) the light produced by hot objects (128)
  luz incandescente la luz producida por los objetos calientes

infrared (in·fruh·RED) electromagnetic wavelengths immediately outside the red end of the visible spectrum (86)
  infrarrojo longitudes de onda electromagnéticas inmediatamente adyacentes al color rojo en el espectro visible

interference (in·ter·FIR·uhns) the combination of two or more waves that results in a single wave (54)
  interferencia la combinación de dos o más ondas que resulta en una sola onda

L

laser (LAY·zer) a device that produces intense light of a narrow range of wavelength and color; laser is an abbreviation of light amplification by stimulated emission of radiation (129)
  láser un dispositivo que produce luz intensa de un rango estrecho de longitud de onda y color; "láser" es una abreviatura de las palabras en inglés "amplificación de luz por emisión estimulada de radiación"

LED (el·ee·DEE) an electronic device that converts electrical energy to light; a light-emitting diode (129)
  LED un dispositivo electrónico que convierte la energía eléctrica en luz; diodo que emite luz

lens (LENZ) a transparent object that refracts light waves such that they converge or diverge to create an image (110)
  lente un objeto transparente que refracta las ondas de luz de modo que converjan o diverjan para crear una imagen

longitudinal wave (lahn·jih·TOOD·n·uhl WAYV) a wave in which the particles of the medium vibrate parallel to the direction of wave motion (8, 38)
  onda longitudinal una onda en la que las partículas del medio vibran paralelamente a la dirección del movimiento de la onda

loudness (LOWD·nes) the extent to which a sound can be heard (43)
  volumen el grado al que se escucha un sonido

M–N

mechanical wave (mih·KAN·ih·kuhl WAYV) a wave that requires a medium through which to travel (10)
  onda mecánica una onda que requiere un medio para desplazarse

medium (MEE·dee·uhm) a physical environment in which phenomena occur; for waves, the material through which a wave can travel (6)
  medio un ambiente físico en el que ocurren fenómenos; para las ondas, el medio a través del cual se desplaza una onda

O

opaque (oh·PAYK) describes an object that is not transparent or translucent (97)
  opaco término que describe un objeto que no es transparente ni translúcido

optical fiber (AHP·tih·kuhl FY·ber) a transparent thread of plastic or glass that transmits light (130)
  fibra óptica un hilo de plástico o vidrio transparente que transmite luz

P–Q

pitch (PICH) a measure of how high or low a sound is perceived to be, depending on the frequency of the sound wave (42)
  altura tonal una medida de qué tan agudo o grave se percibe un sonido, dependiendo de la frecuencia de la onda sonora

R

radiation (ray·dee·AY·shuhn) the transfer of energy as electromagnetic waves (84)
  radiación la transferencia de energía en forma de ondas electromagnéticas

real image (REE·uhl IM·ij) an image that is formed by the intersection of light rays; a real image can be projected on a screen (108)
  imagen real una imagen que se forma por la intersección de rayos de luz; una imagen real se puede proyectar en una pantalla

reflection (rih·FLEK·shuhn) the bouncing back of a ray of light, sound, or heat when the ray hits a surface that it does not go through (97)
  reflexión el rebote de un rayo de luz, sonido o calor cuando el rayo golpea una superficie pero no la atraviesa

refraction (rih·FRAK·shuhn) the bending of a wave front as the wave front passes between two substances in which the speed of the wave differs (100)
  refracción el curvamiento de un frente de ondas a medida que el frente pasa entre dos sustancias en las que la velocidad de las ondas difiere

resonance (REZ·uh·nuhns) a phenomenon that occurs when two objects naturally vibrate at the same frequency; the sound produced by one object causes the other object to vibrate (56)

resonancia un fenómeno que ocurre cuando dos objetos vibran naturalmente a la misma frecuencia; el sonido producido por un objeto hace que el otro objeto vibre

retina (RET·n·uh) the light-sensitive inner layer of the eye, which receives images formed by the lens and transmits them through the optic nerve to the brain (121)

retina la capa interna del ojo, sensible a la luz, que recibe imágenes formadas por el lente ocular y las transmite al cerebro por medio del nervio óptico

scattering (SKAT·er·ing) an interaction of light with matter that causes light to change direction (101)

dispersión la interacción de la luz con la materia que produce un cambio de dirección de la luz

sonar (SOH·nar) sound navigation and ranging, a system that uses acoustic signals and returned echoes to determine the location of objects or to communicate (65)

sonar navegación y exploración por medio del sonido; un sistema que usa señales acústicas y ondas de eco que regresan para determinar la ubicación de los objetos o para comunicarse

sound wave (SOWND WAYV) a longitudinal wave that is caused by vibrations and that travels through a material medium (38)

onda sonora una onda longitudinal que se origina debido a vibraciones y que se desplaza a través de un medio material

translucent (trans·LOO·suhnt) describes matter that transmits light but that does not transmit an image (96)

traslúcido término que describe la materia que transmite luz, pero que no transmite una imagen

transparent (trans·PAIR·uhnt) describes matter that allows light to pass through with little interference (96)

transparente término que describe materia que permite el paso de la luz con poca interferencia

transverse wave (TRANS·vers WAYV) a wave in which the particles of the medium move perpendicularly to the direction the wave is traveling (9)

onda transversal una onda en la que las partículas del medio se mueven perpendicularmente respecto a la dirección en la que se desplaza la onda

ultrasound (UHL·truh·sownd) sound waves with frequencies greater than 20,000 hertz (Hz), the upper limit of typical hearing levels in humans, often used for medical purposes (64)

ultrasonido ondas sonoras con frecuencias mayores de 20,000 hertz (Hz), el límite superior de los niveles de audición típicos en los seres humanos, usadas generalmente con propósitos médicos

ultraviolet (uhl·truh·VY·uh·lit) electromagnetic wave frequencies immediately above the visible range (86)

ultravioleta longitudes de onda electromagnéticas inmediatamente adyacentes al color violeta en el espectro visible

virtual image (VER·choo·uhl IM·ij) an image from which light rays appear to diverge, even though they are not actually focused there; a virtual image cannot be projected on a screen (107)

imagen virtual una imagen en la que los rayos de luz parecen divergir, aunque en realidad no se han centrado allí; una imagen virtual no se puede proyectar en una pantalla

W–Z

wave (WAYV) a disturbance that transfers energy from one place to another; a wave can be a single cycle, or it can be a repeating pattern (6, 18)

onda una alteración que transfiere energía de un lugar a otro; una onda puede ser un ciclo único o un patrón repetido

wave period (WAYV PIR·ee·uhd) the time required for corresponding points on consecutive waves to pass a given point (19)

período de onda el tiempo que se requiere para que los puntos correspondientes de ondas consecutivas pasen por un punto dado

wave speed (WAYV SPEED) the speed at which a wave travels; speed depends on the medium (22)

rapidez de onda la rapidez a la cual viaja una onda; la rapidez depende del medio

wavelength (WAYV·lengkth) the distance from any point on a wave to the corresponding point on the next wave (18)

longitud de onda la distancia entre cualquier punto de una onda y el punto correspondiente de la siguiente onda

Index

Page numbers for definitions are printed in **boldface** type.
Page numbers for illustrations, maps, and charts are printed in *italics*.